TOP **10**
TOKYO

STEPHEN MANSFIELD

I0608431

DK
EYEWITNESS TRAVEL

Left **Game Center, The Ginza** Centre **Ichi no Torii, Meiji Shrine** Right **Kabuki-za Theatre building**

LONDON, NEW YORK,
MELBOURNE, MUNICH AND DELHI
www.dk.com

Design, Editorial and Picture Research by
Quadrum Solutions, Krishnamai, 33B, Sir
Pochkanwala Road, Worli, Mumbai, India

Reproduced by Colourscan, Singapore
Printed and bound in China by
Leo Paper Products Ltd.

First published in Great Britain in 2009 by
Dorling Kindersley Limited, 80 Strand,
London WC2R 0RL, A Penguin Company

**Copyright 2009 © Dorling
Kindersley Limited, London**

A CIP catalogue record is available from
the British Library.

ISBN 978 1 40534 336 7

Within each Top 10 list in this book, no
hierarchy of quality or popularity is implied.
All 10 are, in the editor's opinion,
of roughly equal merit.

We're trying to be cleaner and greener:
• we recycle waste and switch things off
• we use paper from responsibly managed forests whenever possible
• we ask our printers to actively reduce water and energy consumption
• we check out our suppliers' working conditions – they never use child labour
Find out more about our values and best practices at www.dk.com

Contents

Tokyo's Top 10

The information in this DK Eyewitness Top 10 Travel Guide is checked regularly.
Every effort has been made to ensure that this book is as up-to-date as possible at the time of going to press. Some details, however, such as telephone numbers, opening hours, prices, gallery hanging arrangements and travel information are liable to change. The publishers cannot accept responsibility for any consequences arising from the use of this book, nor for any material on third party websites, and cannot guarantee that any website address in this book will be a suitable source of travel information. We value the views and suggestions of our readers very highly. Please write to: Publisher, DK Eyewitness Travel Guides, Dorling Kindersley, 80 Strand, London WC2R 0RL.

Cover: Front – **Alamy Images:** PCL bl; **Getty Images:** Glen Allison main image.
Spine – **DK Images:** Martin Hladik b. Back – **DK Images:** Martin Hladik tc, tl, tr.

Left **Prada Aoyama shop** Centre **Azuma Bridge over the Sumida River** Right **Shinjuku Gyoen**

Left **Cherry blossoms** Right **Benten-do in Ueno Park**

 Key to abbreviations
Adm *admission charge*

TOKYO'S TOP 10

TOKYO'S TOP 10

Tokyo's Highlights

The easternmost of the great Asian cities, Tokyo is a city of perpetual change – one that embraces transformation and fluidity. More interested in the future than the past, it nevertheless carries its history and traditions into the present. This intensely cultural capital is one of the world's most energetic and creative cities. The following ten sights are a must for any first-time visitor, and for those who return to Tokyo, there is always something new to discover.

Imperial Palace Grounds
Part "Forbidden City," part public park, the palace grounds are encircled by moats, stone walls, ancient bridges, keeps, and gardens – elements in the history of the original city *(see pp8–9)*.

Senso-ji Temple
The grounds of this fascinating temple are packed with attractions, which begin at the Thunder Gate and the commercial corridor of Nakamise *(see pp10–11)*.

Sumida River
An excursion starting under its famous bridges is a journey through the history and development of the city *(see pp12–13)*.

Edo-Tokyo Museum
Blending history, art, and architecture, this stupendous museum traces the history of the city from Edo Castle to the Tokyo Olympics *(see pp14–15)*.

Ueno Park
A compendium of Japanese cultural history, this extensive park contains temples, mausoleums, major museums, a zoo, and a splendid lotus pond. With its 1,000 cherry trees, the park serves as a great picnic spot in spring *(see pp16–17)*.

SHINJUKU-KU

Yoyogi · Shinjuku Gyoen Garden · Waka

Sendagaya

Yoyogi Park · Kasumigaokamachi

SHIBUYA-KU · Jingumae · Aoyama Cemetery

Shibuya · Aoyama

Tokyo National Museum
The world's largest collection of Japanese art and archeology plus Chinese, Korean, and Central Asian art treasures are housed here *(see pp18–21)*.

Preceding pages **gates to Gojo and Hanazono Inari Fox Shrines**

Koishikawa Korakuen Garden 7

Tokyo's oldest garden has a heart-shaped pond, lacquered wood and stone bridges, rock arrangements, islands, miniature hills, and a lotus pond – all rife with symbolism *(see pp22–3)*.

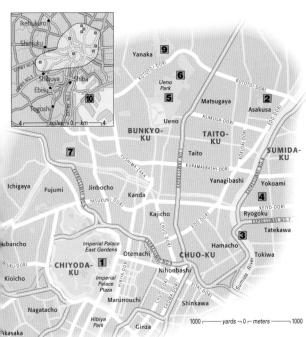

Meiji Shrine 8

At the center of a forest, the exquisite Shinto architecture of shrine buildings and a beautiful iris garden embody the theme of nature *(see pp24–5)*.

Yanaka Cemetery 9

Ghosts of old Edo linger here among the gnarled cherry trees and moldering tombs of shoguns, warriors, writers, and Kabuki actors *(see pp26–7)*.

Odaiba Island 10

Featuring high-tech buildings, exhibition sites, museums, fashion malls, a giant Ferris wheel, and a man-made beach, the artificial island of Odaiba is both enter-tainment and experiment *(see pp28–9)*.

TOP 10 Imperial Palace Grounds

At the center of one of the largest cities in the developed world, the Imperial Palace grounds sit amid a galaxy of busy urban centers. The compound contains the magnificent remains of the emperor's residence, moats, stone walls, watch towers, ancient towers and gates, fairytale bridges, and occasional police cordons. Among the few places where one can witness the persistence of history, the public areas of the grounds are also home to museums, galleries, and beautifully maintained Japanese gardens. A hugely solemn spot, resonating with cultural meaning, the grounds never fail to enthrall visitors.

A picturesque view of the Sakurada-mon Gate

🕐 All the museums here remain closed on Mondays. Try to visit the grounds early, before the mid-morning tour groups turn up. Spring visitors can enjoy the plum and cherry blossom viewing in February and late April, and azaleas and dogwood in mid-May.

🍴 Picnics are permitted in Kitanomaru Park, but it's better to cross the road south of the palace grounds for Hibiya Park, where there is an outdoor café serving sandwiches, noodles, and a surprisingly decent plate of British fish 'n chips.

• Map K1–M4
Chiyoda, Chiyoda-ku
• Adm (for museums and galleries)
• www.kunaicho.go.jp/eindex.html

Top 10 Features

1. Sakurada-mon Gate
2. Nippon Budokan
3. National Museum of Modern Art
4. Imperial Palace Plaza
5. Chidorigafuchi
6. Crafts Gallery
7. Shiomizaka
8. Wadakura Fountain Park
9. Ote-mon Gate and Nijubashi Bridge
10. Imperial Palace East Gardens

Sakurada-mon Gate
This entrance to the palace's outer gardens was erected in 1457. A survivor of earthquakes, fires, and air raids, the entrance consists of two structures: one, a broad inner gate, is angled at 90-degrees to thwart intruders.

Nippon Budokan
The colossal octagonal roof of the Budokan *(left)*, or Japan Martial Arts Hall, has onion-shaped finials covered in gold leaf. Its ornamental elements resemble those seen in traditional Japanese temples.

National Museum of Modern Art
More than 3,000 works by Japanese and Western artists, dating from the Meiji era to the present day, are exhibited here. The controversial Paris habitué Fujita Tsuguhara is also featured.

Imperial Palace Plaza
The plaza's manicured lawns, cherry trees, and stands of ornamental black pine were laid out in 1899. The gravel concourse acts as a firebreak.

The Imperial Palace Plaza's gravel concourse also serves as a cordon sanitaire separating the palace from the city proper.

5 Chidorigafuchi
The stone walls of the shogun's former castle contrast with the inky waters of Chidorigafuchi moat, home to turtles, carp, cormorants, egrets, and gliding swans.

6 Crafts Gallery
This 1910 government listed structure *(above)* once quartered the Imperial Guard. The gallery showcases the works of Japanese craftsmen.

7 Shiomizaka
Stone walls line the path up to the "Tide View Slope." The small promontory once commanded fine views of the sea and Mount Fuji.

8 Wadakura Fountain Park
The sprays and jets of this aquatic park *(above)*, built to commemorate the wedding of the present Emperor and Empress, were refurbished in 1995.

9 Ote-mon Gate and Nijubashi Bridge
South of Ote-mon Gate, the reconstructed 1888 Nijubashi Bridge *(center)* is a graceful span. The bridge, with Fushimi Tower behind, is a popular backdrop for photos.

10 Imperial Palace East Gardens
Designed by Kobori Enshu in the early 17th century, these gardens *(below)* feature stone lanterns, bridges, ponds, swathes of flowers, and towering zelkova trees.

Traumas in the Gardens

The tranquil gardens and concourses of today's palace grounds have known their fair share of drama. Victims of the great 1923 earthquake sheltered here. During the war, several members of Japan's officer corps, inconsolable at news of their nation's defeat, came here in August 1945 to commit ritual suicide. In the 1950s and '60s the plaza witnessed violent political demonstrations.

TOP 10 Senso-ji Temple

Rebuilt countless times since its founding in 628, Senso-ji is the oldest temple site in Tokyo and the capital's spiritual epicenter. The current temple, dedicated to Kannon, the Goddess of Mercy, is a fireproof replica of an earlier version built in 1692. One of the liveliest spots in the city, its grounds attract throngs of visitors who come to pray inside its cavernous main hall with its opulent, golden altar and priceless collection of 18th- and 19th-century votive paintings. This religious sanctuary lies at the heart of a busy commercial and entertainment district. Here, the murmur of chanting sutras, flickering candles, and clouds of incense co-exist with a lively trade in religious souvenirs, trinkets, and traditional foods.

Five-story pagoda in the temple grounds

🕐 The temple grounds can get crowded, so be sure to make an early start on the sights.

Combine a trip to the temple with a river cruise from Azumbashi Bridge.

🍴 Grab an outside table at one of the many local backstreet restaurants to the west of the temple for an early lunch.

• Map R1
• 2-3-1 Asakusa, Taito-ku
• 3844-1575
• Open 24 hrs
• www.senso-ji.jp

Top 10 Features

1. The Thunder Gate
2. Niten-mon Gate
3. Asakusa Jinja
4. Nade Jizo
5. Incense Burner
6. Senso-ji Main Hall
7. Giant Straw Sandals
8. Denbo-in Garden
9. Benten Mound
10. Nakamise

The Thunder Gate
The gate is flanked by two gods: Fujin and Raijin. A red paper lantern with the character for "thunder" emblazoned across it hangs above the gate *(below)*.

Niten-mon Gate
The 1618 ox-blood colored gate is a designated Important Cultural Treasure. Its pillars and walls are covered with votive papers stuck there by the faithful. The gate was recently restored.

Asakusa Jinja
At the entrance to the 1649 shrine's main hall sit protective lion-dog statues, honoring two men who found an image of the goddess Kannon in their fishing nets.

Nade Jizo
This bronze bodhisattva statue *(left)*, a figure of compassion, is believed to relieve ailments if you rub the part of its body that troubles you.

The two fierce-looking meteorological deities flanking the Thunder Gate are Fujin, god of the wind, and Raijin, god of thunder.

5 Incense Burner
A giant bronze incense burner *(left)* stands in front of the main hall. The faithful burn pink sticks of incense, wafting the smoke over their clothes for good luck.

6 Senso-ji Main Hall
Senso-ji has a lavish interior, the centerpiece of which is a richly decorated gold and lacquer altar. Walls have votive paintings and the ceiling has a colorful dragon motif surrounded by angels and lotuses.

7 Giant Straw Sandals
Two large straw sandals *(below)* hang on the walls of the Hozomon Treasury Gate. Made for deities with feet of mythic size, the sandals symbolize the traditional footwear of the Buddhist pilgrim.

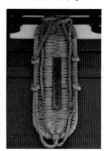

8 Denbo-in Garden
This tranquil garden was designed in the early 1600s by the Zen gardener Kobori Enshu. Tea ceremonies are performed in a small pavilion beside the pond.

9 Benten Mound
Dedicated to Benten, goddess of beauty and the arts, a red shrine sits atop a hill built over an ancient burial mound. A bell rings for the opening of the temple grounds.

Mystery of the Golden Kannon

On March 18, 628, two fishermen brothers found a golden statue of the goddess Kannon in their nets. The 2-inch (5-cm) image is today enshrined in Senso-ji. At the moment of discovery, according to legend, a golden dragon danced from heaven to earth. A Golden Dragon Dance is held in the temple grounds every spring and fall to mark the occasion.

Nakamise
The main avenue to the city's holiest sanctuary is crammed with more than 150 stalls and booths *(right)*, selling a wide range of traditional goods and souvenirs.

Request a pass from the booth next to the five-story pagoda for admittance to Denbo-in Garden.

🔟 Sumida River

The Sumidagawa, Tokyo's premier waterway, has long been a symbol of the city. While its water and embankments are a setting for commerce, festivals, islands, gardens, bridges, and ferries, its literary associations form a rich body of lore. The painted girders, shackles, and bolts of older bridges, with their sweeping arches, stone stanchions, and wrought-iron lanterns, lend a sense of continuity to the ever-changing Tokyo. Low-hulled skulls operated by oarsmen carrying courtesans to riverside teahouses have now given way to water-buses, floating bars, and traditional pleasure boats hung with colorful lanterns.

Komagata Bridge over Sumida River

🚤 The best way to see the river highlights is to take a water bus *(see p117)* between Asakusa and the Hama Rikyu Garden, or a little farther on to Odaiba Island. Enthusiasts of the poet Basho can stroll just north of the Basho Inari Shrine to the Basho Memorial Museum, a research center with a fine collection of manuscripts, calligraphy, and illustrations of scenes from his life.

🍴 Next to Ryogoku JR station, on the opposite bank of the river to Yanagibashi Bridge, Beer Garden Ryogoku is a good lunchtime or afternoon stop for German- and Japanese-style snacks and the company's own microbrew.

Top 10 Features

1. Asahi Beer Hall
2. Komagata Bridge
3. River Fireworks
4. Yanagibashi Bridge
5. Umaya Bridge
6. Basho Inari Shrine and Statue
7. Kiyosu Bridge
8. Eitai Bridge
9. Tsukuda-jima
10. Hama Rikyu Garden

1 Asahi Beer Hall
Frenchman Philippe Starck designed the striking, polished black building *(above)* in the form of an inverted pyramid, looming above Azuma Bridge. Even more surreal is the massive rooftop installation known as the *Flamme d'Or*.

2 Komagata Bridge
The curving blue girders and stone stanchions of this prewar, 1927 bridge combine strength and elegance. The span's eight lanterns are lit at twilight, creating one of the city's most romantic nighttime scenes.

3 River Fireworks
The Japanese call fireworks *hanabi*, meaning "fire flowers." The fireworks show *(below)*, held between Komagata and Umaya bridges, takes place on the last Saturday of July.

Asahi Beer Hall, better known as Asahi Super Dry Hall, was built in 1989 for the Asahi Beer Company.

4 Yanagibashi Bridge

This green bridge *(left)* at the heart of an old geisha district has bolted plates in the southern Chuo ward and north-facing panels in Taito ward. House boats and fishing boats are moored here.

5 Umaya Bridge

This imposing iron structure is named after the shogun's horse stables, once located north of the bridge. Bas-relief horses appear on the ornamental pillars.

6 Basho Inari Shrine and Statue

Dedicated to the great haiku poet Matsuo Basho (1644–94), the shrine leads to a small elevated garden with a seated statue of him *(above)*.

7 Kiyosu Bridge

Built in 1928, this blue bridge *(center)* was inspired by a suspension bridge that once crossed the Rhine in Cologne. The light from the lamps adds to the air of romance.

8 Eitai Bridge

Convicts were once loaded onto boats from this bridge and shipped off to Japan's penal colonies. It offers sweeping scenic river views.

9 Tsukuda-jima

The first residents of this island congregated at the Sumiyoshi Shrine, dedicated to Sumiyoshi Myojin, protector of seafarers.

River Chronicles

The writings of Tokyo's foremost chronicler, the novelist Nagai Kafu (1879–1959), are evocative descriptions of the city. Kafu's river is a leisurely waterway, supporting a population in tune with the seasons. In an early novel, *The Sumida River*, Kafu presents a vibrant portrait of the river with a miniaturist's eye. His later elegies lament the changes carried out in the name of progress.

10 Hama Rikyu Garden

The features of the original garden *(above)* can be seen in the tidal pond, in islets linked by wooden bridges, and in a tea pavilion. Sluice gates let seawater enter the pond, bringing in saltwater fish.

The Tsukuda-jima island's first inhabitants were brought from Osaka to supply the shogun's kitchens with whitebait.

🔟 Edo-Tokyo Museum

Charting the history of Edo and Tokyo, the Edo-Tokyo Museum is housed in an elevated building that resembles an intergalactic space station floating on stilts. Its height, which dwarfs every other building in the vicinity, replicates Edo Castle, and the raised edifice is modeled after a traditional Japanese rice storehouse. More modern touches include the red escalator that rises from the terrace to the underbelly of the cantilevered upper stories, and the panels coated with fluorine resin. Highlights include a replica of Nihonbashi Bridge and an evocative reconstruction of the 1945 air raids that ravaged Tokyo.

Entranceway, Edo-Tokyo Museum

🎧 A small, refundable deposit is required for borrowing earphones that provide audio commentary. Volunteer guides are available for tours in English, French, German, Spanish, Chinese, and other languages. Call the museum at least two weeks in advance to reserve a guide.

☕ Coffee House Café Cardenas on the seventh floor serves tea, cold drinks, and light snacks.

- Map H3
- 1-4-1 Yokoami, Sumida-ku
- 3626-9974
- Ryogoku, Hanzomon subway, JR Sobu line
- Open 9:30am Tue, Wed, Fri–Sun; 9:30am–7:30pm Thu
- Adm
- www.edo-tokyo-museum.or.jp

Top 10 Features

1. Westernization
2. Photos of Edo-Meiji Periods
3. Portable Festival Floats
4. Daimyo Lodgings
5. Districts
6. Kabuki Theater
7. Row House Tenement
8. Woodblock Printing
9. Nihonbashi Bridge
10. Life of Craftsmen and Townspeople

1 Westernization
Tokyo's experiment at assimilating Western trends is visible in the fifth-floor models of early buildings designed by European architects and engineers *(above)*. Prewar culture is represented in themes such as "The Rise of the Working Woman."

2 Photos of Edo-Meiji Periods
By the Meiji era (1868–1912), sepia-toned images of samurais and rickshaw pullers became outdated. These gave way to photographs of Western-style hotels, trams, exhibition sites, and factories along Sumida River.

3 Portable Festival Floats
The exquisite *omikoshi (below)* are crafted for use during traditional festivals. These portable shrines are lacquered, gold-plated, and encrusted with precious stones.

Daimyo Lodgings
4 The sixth-floor model *(above)* of the grand estates of *daimyo* (feudal lords) was skillfully reconstructed from old prints and plans.

Districts
5 Models on the sixth floor show the Edo-era residential districts. The fifth floor showcases villages and river islands connected to Edo.

Kabuki Theater
6 This superb replica of the Nakamura-za Kabuki theater recreates stage scenes from the mid-17th century. The stage is animated by life-size models *(center)* of Kabuki's all-male actors in gorgeous robes, wigs, and hair ornaments.

Row House Tenement
7 Today's living conditions may be cramped, but during the Edo period townspeople had to make do with inconceivably small homes *(above)*. An example of a typical tenement row house can be seen on the fifth floor.

Woodblock Printing
8 Lifesize re-creations of a printing shop and Edo-era bookstore on the fifth floor are complemented by display cases containing printing equipment, books, and samples of woodblock prints *(right)* popular at the time.

Nihonbashi Bridge
9 The sixth floor leads directly onto a reconstructed section of Nihonbashi Bridge. The carpentry and joinery of the original bridge, which was rebuilt several times, can be seen in the replica.

Life of Craftsmen and Townspeople
10 The life of ordinary people can be seen in the seventh-floor models of townspeople's residences, and the well-crafted mock-ups of the commercial city on the fifth floor.

Museum Guide

Ticket counters are on the second floor beneath the main building, and outside on the third-floor terrace to the left of the main building. An escalator takes visitors to the permanent exhibitions on the fifth and sixth floors. The sixth floor focuses on the Edo-period city, and the fifth on Edo's later years and transition to Tokyo. Descend to the first floor for special exhibitions and the impressive museum store. There is also a Sumida ward souvenir store featuring local crafts.

During the Edo period (1603–1867) the social classes were allocated districts according to their trade and status.

🔟 Ueno Park

One of the most important concentrations of high art in the city, Ueno Park sits at the center of a down-to-earth working-class residential and entertainment district. With its temples, shrines, famous cherry trees, a magnificent lotus pond, statues, and tombs, the park is like a miniature model of Japan. The hill, on which the upper part of the park sits, was once a great religious center. During the Meiji and Taisho periods, this historical stage served as a venue for large-scale art and industrial exhibitions, paving the way for the venerable museums and galleries that occupy the park today. Almost all of Tokyo gathers here during the enchanting spring cherry-blossom season.

Visitors outside the Shitamachi Museum

🎨 Those interested in art can combine a visit to the park with the nearby Taikan Yokoyama Memorial Hall *(see p84)*, the painter's private house and lovely garden.

🍴 Buy a drink from one of the vending machines beside the outdoor tables in front of Benten Island. The café here has inexpensive light dishes, such as fried noodles.

- Map F1
- Ueno Koen, Taito-ku
- Open 24 hrs

Top 10 Features

1. Toshogu Shrine and Kara-mon Gate
2. Benten-do
3. Gojo Tenjinsha and Hanazono Inari Fox Shrines
4. Saigo Takamori Statue
5. Shitamachi Museum
6. Ueno Zoo
7. Five-Story Pagoda
8. National Museum of Western Art
9. Shinobazu Pond
10. Cherry Trees

1 Toshogu Shrine and Kara-mon Gate

This opulently decorated shrine *(above)*, dedicated to the memory of the first shogun, Ieyasu, was renovated in 1651. A row of stone and copper lanterns leads to the shrine.

2 Benten-do

This temple honors the Goddess of Beauty, often depicted playing a four-stringed lute. The ceiling inside the hall is painted with dragons, and the walls with murals of fall flowers.

3 Gojo Tenjinsha and Hanazono Inari Fox Shrines

Winding paths lead through red *torii* gates to Gojo and Hanazono shrines. Inside stand Inari fox statues *(below)*.

The stone and copper lanterns at the Toshogu Shrine were donated by warlords eager to curry favor with the shogun.

4 Saigo Takamori Statue

The bronze statue *(left)*, unveiled in 1898, is a tribute to Takamori, a powerful samurai who led a major rebellion in the 19th century. He is shown wearing a summer kimono, walking his dog.

5 Shitamachi Museum

Displaying everyday items such as kitchenware and furniture, this museum also features re-creations of Edo-era stores and tenements *(see p84)*.

6 Ueno Zoo

Built in 1882, the zoo is home to pandas, snow leopards, Bengal tigers, and bison. A short mono-rail ride leads to a petting section. The range of critters here is impressive.

7 Five-Story Pagoda

Covered with bronze roof tiles to protect it from fire, the current pagoda *(above)* was built in 1640. The 120-ft (37-m) tall vermillion structure stands inside the zoo.

8 National Museum of Western Art

The original 1959 design was by Le Corbusier. Exhibits range from 15th-century religious portraits to works by the likes of Miro and Pollack.

9 Shinobazu Pond

The pond's southern section is filled with pink lotuses in the summer. A clump of reeds provides a habitat for herons, black-headed gulls, grebes, and spot-billed ducks.

10 Cherry Trees

Every spring, the park plays host to Tokyo's largest cherry blossom party *(right)*. Beer, sake, and impromptu karaoke songs and dance are the main highlights.

Meiji Restoration

A fierce battle between supporters of the deposed shogun and the new forces of the Meiji restoration was fought on Ueno Hill in 1868. Heavy rains flooded Shinobazu Pond, with men combating in knee-deep water, while a cannon shot from a tea-house on one side of the water and another from a cave dedicated to Inari exploded over their heads. More than 300 men died in the conflict.

Tokyo National Museum

Occupying a major part of the northern reaches of Ueno Park, the colossal Tokyo National Museum was known in the prewar period as the Imperial Household Museum. This magisterial museum, set among courtyards, fountains, and trees, is divided into four main galleries: Honkan, Heiseikan, Toyokan, and Horyu-ji. These contain not only the single-most important collection of Japanese art and archeology in the world, but a treasury of Asian antiquities as well. The main galleries display almost 3,000 items at any one time – an awesome amount to see in one visit.

Elegant exterior of the Honkan Gallery

⊘ The excellent museum shop in the basement of the Honkan sells items linked to museum exhibits and motifs.

⊖ The Hotel Okura's garden terrace in the Horyu-ji Gallery is a pleasant, airy, upscale setting for a set lunch. There are cheaper food and drink options at the stalls and cafés in Ueno Park.

- Map F1
- 13-9 Ueno koen, Taito-ku
- 3822-1111
- Open 9:30am–5pm, Tue–Sun
- Adm
- www.tnm.jp

Top 10 Features
1. Arms and Armor
2. Japanese Archeology
3. Ceramics
4. Asian Arts
5. Lacquerware
6. Calligraphy
7. Horyu-ji Treasures
8. Japanese Paintings and Prints
9. Textiles
10. Religious Sculpture

Arms and Armor
The equipment once owned by the country's military elite is displayed in the Honkan. This includes the warriors' attire *(above)*: armor, helmets, saddlery, and sword mountings.

Japanese Archeology
The Heiseikan, dedicated to Japanese archeology, houses relics *(left)* from the ancient Jomon period (c.10,000–300 BC) onward. The chronology of Japanese arts can be found here.

Ceramics
Japanese ceramics *(above)* in the Honkan are represented by work from Kyoto and Imari ware. The Toyokan has Chinese ceramics from the Song to Qing dynasties, and some beautifully glazed Ming dynasty work.

The Honkan's ceramics collection also features objects made for the tea ceremony, including some fine Korean tea bowls.

Asian Arts
4 The Toyokan *(above)* is the place to go for Asian arts. Exhibits include ancient bronze drums, Korean metalwork, textiles, Khmer pottery, Hindu statuary, and cave paintings from the grottoes of Xingling.

Japanese Paintings and Prints
8 The Honkan features paintings from the classical Heian to Muromachi periods, as well as fine examples of mural, screen, and paper door art, and Zen-inspired ink landscapes *(center)*. The highlight of the Edo era is the work of its *ukiyo-e* woodblock print artists.

Textiles
9 The Toyokan has a sumptuous collection of textiles from China, Korea, Southeast Asia, India, the Middle East, and Egypt. Exquisite Indonesian brocade work made from gold thread can also be seen here. The Honkan Gallery houses Japanese textiles.

Religious Sculpture
10 Religious sculptures *(left)* are scattered throughout the galleries. Bronze, gilt, and sandstone sculptures from Pakistan are exhibited in the Toyokan. The Honkan displays Buddhist statues from India and Japan.

Lacquerware
5 Included among the Japanese National Treasures and Important Cultural Properties in the Honkan Gallery are *maki-e* lacquerware items dating from the Heian to Edo periods.

Calligraphy
6 The master calligraphy in the Honkan includes *bokuseki*, calligraphy executed by Zen priests. Even if the meanings of the Chinese characters elude you, the beauty of the brushwork won't.

Horyu-ji Treasures
7 These invaluable art works *(above)*, including a forest of standing bodhisattvas from the Horyu-ji Temple, are now exhibited in the Gallery of Horyu-ji Treasures.

Museum Guide
The main gate to the museum complex, consisting of four major galleries, lies at the north end of Ueno Park. The central gallery, the Honkan, is straight ahead, beyond the pond and fountains. The Toyokan is on the right, the Heiseikan to the left, behind the Honkan. The Gallery of Horyu-ji Treasures lies to the left of the main gate, behind the Hyokeikan, a grand building used for special exhibits and educational events.

Tokyo's Top 10

Look out for gold and mother-of-pearl inlay work on cosmetic boxes and fans among the Honkan's lacquerware collection.

19

Left **Honkan** Right **Azekura Sutra Store**

Top 10 Outdoor Features

1 Honkan
The elegant main gallery and centerpiece of Ueno Park was designed by Jin Watanabe. It was built in 1938 in the so-called "Imperial Crown" style of architecture. The features are Japanese, but the building materials are undeniably Western.

2 Toyokan
Asian artworks and archeology are housed in a light, modernist building designed by Taniguchi Yoshiro, but the raised porch and overhanging roof finials are more suggestive of Buddhist temples.

3 Hyokeikan
Built in 1909, the Hyokeikan is a highly prized example of a Meiji-era Western-style building. The white stone walls and green domes of this Important Cultural Property are impressive.

Display, Gallery of Horyu-ji Treasures

Green-domed Hyokeikan

4 Heiseikan
The wide open courtyard in front of the building, auditorium, and lounge speak of contemporary architecture and planning, whereas its pottery, burial statues, and broken shards are of the ancient world.

5 Gallery of Horyu-ji Treasures
The minimalist 1999 design of this gallery is the work of Yoshio Taniguchi, whose overseas projects include the ground-breaking Museum of Modern Art (MOMA) in New York.

6 Shiryokan
The Shiryokan is a research and information center, where visitors can browse through archives, books, magazines, monochrome and color photographs, and other materials linked to art history.

7 The Black Gate
A rare structure from the Edo period, the Kuromon is topped with a heavy hip-and-gable style roof. Old roof tiles and foundation stones are kept in the rear of the gate, adding to the air of antiquity.

8 Azekura Sutra Store
Buddhist sutras were once kept in stores like this one, transported in 1881 from Gango-ji temple in Nara. Constructed of

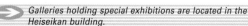
Galleries holding special exhibitions are located in the Heiseikan building.

Top 10 Asian Art Themes

1. Indian and Gandharan Sculpture (13th–2nd century BC)
2. Ancient Asian Bronze Drums (6th–5th century BC)
3. West Asian Textiles (19th century AD)
4. Chinese Archeology (2nd–1st century BC)
5. Chinese Textiles (15th–17th century AD)
6. Chinese Ceramics (Three Kingdoms period –Tang Dynasty)
7. Chinese Ceramics (Song –Qing Dynasty)
8. Chinese Stone Reliefs from Shangdong (1st–2nd century)
9. Korean Ceramics (9th–10th century)
10. Central Asian Religious Cave Paintings (Tang Dynasty)

Asian Art Themes

With roughly 110,000 objects in its collection, the Tokyo National Museum regularly rotates its exhibits. The themes listed here at the Toyokan are part of its permanent collection, but individual displays change. Since the Toyokan is currently undergoing renovation, the Asian works will be exhibited in alternative rooms.

Left **Indian sculpture** Right **Chinese ceramic**

Stone Age Tokyo

Early settlers lived along the ridges and bluffs of the present-day Yamanote Hills. The elevated ground gave them access to plentiful supplies of fish. The pre-Bronze Age site – the Omori Shell Mound – in Western Tokyo was discovered in 1877 by the American zoologist Edward Sylvester Morse. The event marked the beginning of Japanese archeology.

logs, the inner walls of this tiny storehouse are decorated with murals depicting bodhisattvas and protective deities.

Statue of Edward Jenner

9 Museum Garden and Teahouses

The site is open to the public during the spring cherry blossom or fall leaf-viewing seasons. Those who happen to be in Tokyo around this time should not pass up the chance to see this secret pond-garden and teahouses on the north side of the Honkan.

10 Statue of Edward Jenner

British physician Edward Jenner (1749–1823) discovered a smallpox vaccine providing immunity against smallpox. This memorial statue by the sculptor Koun Takamura was erected as a tribute to Jenner in 1896.

TOP 10 Koishikawa Korakuen Garden

Laid out in 1629, Tokyo's oldest surviving garden was commissioned by Tokugawa Yorifusa, lord of the Mito branch of the Tokugawa family. Its designer, Tokudaiji Sahei, was aided by the Confucian scholar, Zhu Shunshui, a Chinese refugee from the fall of the Ming dynasty. Many famous spots found in China and Japan have been re-created in miniature here. The garden was once a kind of theme park itself, a recreational space for the Tokugawa clan to entertain visitors, clamber up its miniature hills, float in barges on its pond, and stage poetry parties.

Verdant rice field, ideal for taking tea

🕐 Try to get to the garden when it opens at 9am, before the amusement park next door gets into full swing. In the fierce summer months the garden is much cooler at this time as well.

🍵 Kantoku-tei, a teahouse with a room facing onto Oigawa River, serves *omatcha* (powdered green tea) along with a traditional Japanese sweet.

• Map E2
• 1-6-6 Koraku, Bunkyo-ku
• 3811-3015
• Open 9am–5pm
• Adm

Top 10 Features

1. Tsuiji Walls
2. Rozan Mountain and Lotuses
3. Symbolic Rice Field
4. Tsutenkyo Bridge
5. Engetsukyo Bridge
6. Kuhachiya House
7. Horai-jima Island
8. Iris Garden
9. Inner Garden
10. Plum Orchards and Yatsu-hashi

1 Tsuiji Walls

The current wall is a reinforced concrete imitation of the original *tsuiji* plaster walls, but moss and staining from Tokyo's steamy summers have given the newer walls a patina of age.

2 Rozan Mountain and Lotuses

Miniature landscapes recalled famous places in poetry and mythology. Below this imitation of Mount Lu in China *(above)* is a sacred lotus pond.

3 Symbolic Rice Field

Created to show the hardships faced by peasant farmers, a rice field lies to the north of the garden. Elementary school children plant and harvest the crop.

4 Tsutenkyo Bridge

Spanning a deep gorge and supported on piles, the bridge *(center)* is a replica of a structure in Tofuku-ji, an important temple complex in Kyoto. Its reflection in the waters of the shallow river below amplifies its size.

Engetsukyo Bridge
A stroll along the winding, tree sheltered paths lead to the Chinese-style Engetsukyo *(above)*, the "round moon bridge," arguably the oldest ornamental stone bridge in Tokyo.

Entrance *Koishikawa Korakuen*

Kuhachiya House
Standing in the middle of a glade of red pines, this thatched-roof building is modeled on an Edo-era drinking house. The original structure, destroyed in the war, was rebuilt in 1959.

Horai-jima Island
The island at the pond's center represents the Taoist paradise of Horai-jima. The idea of placing a "heavenly isle" in a garden was first conceived by the Chinese Emperor Wu Di.

Iris Garden
Planted in the marsh surrounding the zigzag bridge, purple and white Japanese and rabbit-ear irises bloom *(below)* during the June rainy season. An ancient system of sluice gates and dikes irrigates the marsh.

Inner Garden
Apart from a long-gone Chinese gate, everything else remains the same as when the Mito family used this Chinese-style inner garden *(below)* as a place of study.

Japanese Tea Ceremony

The dual purpose of the ceremony is to create a spirit of modesty and to express deep hospitality to tea guests. Stepping stones leading to the teahouse are designed to slow down guests, to decrease the pace of ordinary life, while the very low entrance requires guests to stoop, a gesture of humility that places everyone on an equal social footing.

Plum Orchards and Yatsu-hashi
An attractive plum orchard just to the north of the pond comes into fragrant white blossom in early February. Nearby, a zigzag, eight-span *yatsuhashi* bridge runs through a small marsh.

Green tea was introduced to Japan in the 12th century when seeds were brought from China and grown in the hills around Uji.

TOP 10 Meiji Shrine

Dedicated to the memory of the Meiji Emperor (1868–1912) and his consort Shoken, Meiji shrine is a fine example of restrained Shinto architecture. Completed in 1920, the shrine was destroyed in an air raid in 1945. The current reconstruction is indistinguishable from the original. The gravel paths and courtyards of the grounds host cultural events, ranging from Noh, Kyogen, court dances, and music performances to horseback archery, winter ice sculptures, and calligraphy shows.

Ichi no Torii
The 36-ft (11-m) gate *(above)* is Japan's largest *torii*. It was built from 1,600-year-old Japanese *hinoki* cypress trees transported from Alishan Mountain in Taiwan.

Visitors buying omikuji, fortune-telling paper strips

🔆 Sensible shoes are recommended for the shrine, a ten-minute walk along a gravel path.

🔵 The boundary of adjacent Yoyogi Park *(see p47)* has many stalls selling Japanese snacks, light meals, hot dogs, and refreshments.

• Map B5
• 1-1 Yoyogi-Kamizonocho, Shibuya-ku
• 3379-5511
• Harajuku, Harajuku JR Yamanote line, Meiji-Jingumae, Chiyoda subway
• Meiji Shrine: open dawn to dusk; Meiji Shrine Iris Garden: open 9am–5pm; Imperial Treasure House: open Sat–Sun, national holidays, festival days
• Adm (for Meiji Shrine Iris Garden and Imperial Treasure House)

Top 10 Features

1. Ichi no Torii
2. Main Shrine
3. Second Torii
4. Meiji Shrine Iris Garden
5. Votive Tablets
6. Imperial Treasure House
7. JR Bridge
8. Traditional Wedding Processions
9. Evergreen Forest
10. Souvenir Store

Main Shrine
This understated yet elegant shrine *(center)* reflects the classic Shinto style in its oxidized roofs, hanging banners, and pillars of cypress and camphor.

Second Torii
This gate signals a left turn into the Inner Garden. *Torii* (gates) symbolize the perch on which a mythological cock sat before it announced the dawn that lured the sun goddess Amaterasu from her cave.

Meiji Shrine Iris Garden
A wooded path leads into a sunken garden *(below)*, bordered by misty woods and thatched gazebos. In early June, purple, pink, and white irises bloom in the water garden.

The 16-petal chrysanthemum medallions on the top bar of Ichi no Torii are a symbol of the imperial family.

Votive Tablets

Ema (votive tablets) are still popular today, especially among students petitioning for divine help in passing exams. Another *ema* is usually hung in gratitude, if a wish is fulfilled *(right)*.

Imperial Treasure House

This collection of personal artifacts belongs to the Meiji royalty. A painting by the Italian artist Ugolini depicts the emperor in European military dress, with a vase standing on a table at his side. In the museum, the same vase stands next to the painting.

JR Bridge

The bridge leading to the shrine is a free zone for performance artists, some who enjoy dressing up as their favorite manga or anime characters, in Rococo hairstyles and Gothic makeup *(below)*.

The Meiji Emperor

In 1867, two British emissaries, Sir Harry Parkes and Algernon Mitford, were granted an audience with the 15-year-old Emperor in his palace in Kyoto. What they found was a vision of medieval sovereignty: a boy dressed in white brocade and vermilion silk trousers, his teeth lacquered black, eyebrows shaved, and cheeks painted red. Less than a year later, he would proclaim the Meiji era. By the end of his reign, Japan was an industrialized nation, strong enough to have defeated Russia in 1904–5.

Traditional Wedding Processions

Along with the many rituals and dedicatory ceremonies held at the shrine, Shinto-style weddings *(right)* are quietly formal in manner and attire, but visually dazzling. Most weddings take place on Saturday afternoons.

Evergreen Forest

Much of the shrine grounds are densely forested. More than 120,000 trees and shrubs create a garden of Japanese horticulture.

Souvenir Store

Amulets, incense, talismans, lucky arrows, key rings strung with a tiny shrine bell, and models of Tanuki (badger deity) are sold here.

10 Yanaka Cemetery

One of Tokyo's first public graveyards, Yanaka Cemetery is an elegiac yet awe-inspiring evocation of Tokyo's past. Its consecrated grounds, interspersed with mossy tombstones, leafy walks, wrought-iron gates, time-worn lanterns, and stone statuary, are almost Gothic in character. An oasis of calm frozen in time, Yanaka Cemetery is a far cry from Tokyo's glittering metropolis. It is also the final resting place of the city's luminaries, including literati, actors, and statesmen, as well as the notorious and the long-forgotten.

Stone lanterns, Yanaka Cemetery

🌀 Ask at the police box for a copy of the *Chomeijin Bochi Annai-zu* (Guide to Famous Graves). It is in Japanese, but the officer on duty will be happy to mark the graves you wish to see.

❓ Retire to nearby Yanaka Ginza, a narrow street of craft shops, small restaurants, and cafés. At the entrance, Chaho Kanekichi-en is an old-fashioned tea shop. Try their Yanaka Midori, a refreshing mix of roasted tea stems and *omatcha* (powdered green tea).

• Map F1

Top 10 Features

1. Tenno-ji Temple
2. Grave of Kazuo Hasegawa
3. Site of Former Five-Tiered Pagoda
4. Bodhisattva, Kannon, and Jizo Stones
5. Train Spotting
6. Shogun Yoshinobu's Grave
7. Resting Place of a Murderess
8. Five-Tiered Tombs
9. Two Women Writers
10. Cherry Blossom Viewing

1 Tenno-ji Temple
This 1274 temple *(above)* is centered around a large seated Buddha statue. The spacious compound is full of colorful hydrangeas, azalea, and magnolia trees.

3 Site of Former Five-Tiered Pagoda
In 1957, two distressed lovers decided to commit suicide here, setting the pagoda on fire. Only traces of the 1644 pagoda remain.

2 Grave of Kazuo Hasegawa
Kazuo Hasegawa (1908–84) was a legendary Japanese actor. Those about to undertake roles played by him visit the grave to petition his spirit for support.

4 Bodhisattva, Kannon, and Jizo Stones
The cemetery is a fine gallery of religious statuary. There are carvings of bodhisattvas *(left)*; Kannon, the Goddess of Mercy; and Jizo, guardian of unborn children and travelers.

5 Train Spotting
As Japan Rail trains zip past the steep banks of Nippori station, one can get a great view from the edge of the cemetery *(above)*. Several lines, including the tracks of the bullet train, run in parallel here.

6 Shogun Yoshinobu's Grave
The last shogun, Tokugawa Yoshinobu (1837–1913), is interred here. Entrance to the grounds of his tomb *(below)* is forbidden, but it is possible to peer over the iron railings that protect it.

7 Resting Place of a Murderess
The grave of Oden Takahashi, murderess of many men, lies at the very edge of the cemetery, as if the authorities were not quite sure whether to include her here or not.

8 Five-Tiered Tombs
Christian headstones stand beside Shinto-style tombs, but the largest number of gravestones are Buddhist. *Gorin-to* are distinctive five-tiered stones, the layers representing earth, water, fire, wind, and heaven.

9 Two Women Writers
Two women novelists, Ichiyo Higuchi (1872–96), whose face appears on the ¥5,000 note, and Fumiko Enchi (1905–86), who wrote novels about female psychology, are buried here.

10 Cherry Blossom Viewing
During spring, the main road through the grave-yard turns into a tunnel of pink blossom *(left)*. Picnickers forego the karaoke sets that blight other blossom-viewing parties. However, plenty of good-natured, tipsy revelers can be expected.

Great Buddha of Yanaka
There may be larger statues in Japan, but Tokyoites have a special affection for their very own Great Buddha of Yanaka. The 16-ft (5-m) statue belongs to Tenno-ji Temple, a sanctuary that was damaged during the Battle of Ueno (1868). The fact that the statue survived added to its mystic appeal and authority. Cast in bronze in 1690, this Chinese-style figure has finely carved facial features, representing the Shaka-nyorai Buddha. It stands in a tranquil corner of the temple precincts, among lush surroundings.

TOP 10 Odaiba Island

When coastal mega-cities run out of space, they inevitably turn toward the sea. An aerial view of Tokyo reveals a city stretched to its limits, coming to a congested stop at the waterfront. Geometrically precise islands appear, seemingly lowered into place like space panels. Among the exhibition pavilions, indoor shopping malls, game centers, cafés, restaurants, and surrealistic constructions of Odaiba Island, the visitor never fails to be intrigued by the structures on this landfill that seem to hail from the future rather than the past.

1 Oedo Onsen Monogatari

Dip into tepid to scalding natural spring waters, indoor and outdoor tubs, a steaming sand bath, sauna, foot massage pool, or bed of hot stones at this spring *(above)*.

Exterior of the Aqua City building

🕐 The island is packed on the weekends. Visit on a weekday.

🍺 Try the Decks Tokyo Brewery's micro-beer. For something lighter, try the Thé Chinois Madu, a teahouse in Venus Fort.

• Map D2 • Oedo Onsen Monogatari: 2-57 Omi, Koto-ku; 5500-1126; 11am–9pm; adm • Tokyo Big Sight: 3-21-2 Ariake, Koto-ku; 5530-1111 • MegaWeb: 1 Aomi, Koto-ku; open 11am–9pm • Fuji TV Building: 2-4-8 Daiba, Minato-ku; 5500-8888; open 10am–8pm Tue–Sun; adm • Museum of Maritime Science: 3-1 Higashi-Yashio, Shinagawa-ku; 5500-1111; open 10am–5pm; adm • National Museum of Emerging Science and Innovation: 2-41 Aomi, Koto-ku; 03-3570-9151; open 10am–5pm Mon, Wed–Sun; adm

Top 10 Features

1. Oedo Onsen Monogatari
2. Tokyo Big Sight
3. Decks and Aqua City
4. MegaWeb
5. Fuji TV Building
6. Carbon Fiber Garden
7. Museum of Maritime Science
8. Palette Town
9. National Museum of Emerging Science and Innovation
10. Rainbow Bridge

2 Tokyo Big Sight

The megalithic exhibition center *(above)* has an eighth-floor Observation Bar Lounge. The gravity-defying structure consists of four inverted pyramids standing on a seemingly narrow base.

3 Decks and Aqua City

Decks is a wooden boulevard of outdoor patios, cafés, and restaurants. Aqua City next door has restaurants, cinema, a video arcade, and theater.

4 MegaWeb

Test-drive new models, enjoy simulated rides, or visit an automobile museum at the Toyota-run MegaWeb *(left)*, the world's biggest car showroom.

One of the highlights of the Decks is Sega Joyopolis, a virtual reality arcade.

Dai-san Daiba
Historical Park

Kokusai-tenjijo

Tokyo
Teleport

Shiokaze
Park

Fuji TV Building
5 Two blocks of this Kenzo Tange-designed building *(below)* are joined by girder-like sky corridors and a titanium-paneled sphere, making it resemble a hi-vision, wide-screen TV set.

Carbon Fiber Garden
6 Cantilevered over a polished marble base, the sculptured garden *(center)* was made from carbon fiber and illuminated rods. It was conceived by Makoto Sei Watanabe.

Museum of Maritime Science
7 This outstanding museum traces the development of shipping and ocean transportation. A simulation of the 1920s Tokyo waterfront is complete with chandler's stores and perspiring stevedores.

Palette Town
8 Palette Town, a complex of stores, showrooms, and amusements, is home to Venus Fort, a designer shopping mall *(below)* with a stunning interior.

National Museum of Emerging Science and Innovation
9 Housed in a futuristic building, this museum focuses on space, life sciences *(below)*, and cutting-edge technologies.

Rainbow Bridge
10 At night this graceful bridge is illuminated against the backdrop of a huge Ferris wheel. Fireworks displays are held on the waters around the bridge's stanchions in the summer.

Defending the Bay
Man-made islands were built as cannon batteries by the Edo-era Tokugawa government to protect Tokyo from foreign invasion. The fear was well founded. In the 1850s, heavily armed American steamships, led by Commodore Perry, moored close offshore *(see p32)*. In all, five islands were built. Today, only Battery Island No. 3 and 6 remain.

Left **Clean-up at the Aum Shinrikyo Subway** Right **Senso-ji Temple**

Top 10 Moments in History

1 Founding of Senso-ji Temple
Discovered by two fishermen in their nets in 628, the golden image of the goddess Kannon was enshrined at the site of present-day Senso-ji. The temple has been rebuilt several times, and after air raids in 1945, a replica was put up in ferro-concrete.

2 Ota Dokan's Fort
The Musashino Plain was developed into a martial domain with the arrival of Ota Dokan, a minor feudal lord, in 1456. Dokan's fortress was built on a site named Edo, meaning "estuary mouth." A statue of the city founder stands at the Tokyo International Forum in Yurakucho.

3 Founding of Edo
The development of Edo village into Japan's de-facto military capital began with the shogun Tokugawa Ieyasu's arrival in 1603. The land was reclaimed, water courses expanded, residences built, and a massive citadel, the Edo Castle, was erected.

4 The Long-Sleeves Fire
In 1657 priests at Hommyo-ji Temple in Hongo tried to burn a kimono worn by a lovelorn girl who died shortly after putting it on. A gust of wind tore it away, starting fresh fires that claimed the lives of over 100,000 people.

5 47 Ronin Incident
In 1701 Lord Asano was ordered to commit ritual suicide for drawing his sword at court. His retainers, who had become *ronin*, or masterless samurai, avenged Asano's death by killing his opponent, Lord Kira, and placing his decapitated head on their master's grave. The act led the authorities to order the 47 loyal retainers to commit suicide.

6 Perry's "Black Ships"
On July 8, 1853, Commodore Matthew Galbraith Perry sailed four heavily armed ships into Edo Bay, to open Japan to diplomatic and trade relations. The "black ships" were a display of superior Western technology, a reminder of the progress that had bypassed the country.

7 Great Kanto Earthquake
At 11:58am on September 1, 1923, as people were preparing lunch on charcoal braziers and gas burners, an earthquake measuring 7.9 on the

An artistic impression of Commodore Perry's "black ships"

Preceding pages **Azaleas in bloom, Ome Garden**

Richter scale convulsed the city. An estimated 100,000 people were crushed or burned to death, and 45 percent of the buildings were destroyed. Few traces of the past remained.

8 Tokyo Air Raids
US raids on Tokyo during WWII exacted a heavy toll on civilian lives. Tokyo suffered 102 raids in all, the worst on the night of March 9–10, 1945, when over 300 B-29 bombers loaded with oil, jellied gasoline, and napalm, swooped over tightly packed residential areas to the east, killing between 80,000 and 100,000 civilians.

Controversial author Yukio Mishima

9 Suicide of Mishima
In 1970 author and right-winger Yukio Mishima took over an upstairs office at the Self-Defense Headquarter and called for the restoration of the emperor. Having failed in his coup, he committed ritual disembowelment in the samurai tradition.

10 Aum Shinrikyo Subway Attack
On March 20, 1995, members of the death cult Aum Shinrikyo, under orders from their leader, Asahara Shoko, placed plastic bags containing liquid sarin gas on the floor of carriages on five subway lines. Twelve passengers died and hundreds were injured.

Top 10 Famous Tokyoites

1 Katsushika Hokusai
Woodblock artist Hokusai (1760–1849) published 30,000 sketches and 500 books.

2 Natsumi Soseki
Regarded by many as Japan's greatest writer, Soseki (1867–1916) set several of his novels in Tokyo.

3 Yukio Mishima
The controversial writer (1925–70) completed his tetralogy, *The Sea of Fertility*, on the day of his death.

4 Junichiro Tanizaki
Tanizaki (1886–1965) explored themes of sexuality, Western modernity, and materialism in his novels.

5 Nagai Kafu
A fine chronicler of the Tokyo demi-monde, Kafu (1879–1959) traced the transformation of the city.

6 Ichiyo Higuchi
The face of the prodigious writer Higuchi (1872–96), who died from tuberculosis, graces the ¥5,000 Japanese note.

7 Yasujiro Ozu
Legendary film director Ozu (1903–63) described the collapse of the Japanese family in *Tokyo Story*.

8 Akira Kurosawa
Kurosawa (1910–98), Japan's best-known film auteur, has inspired Stephen Spielberg and George Lucas.

9 Yoko Ono
Ono (b. 1933) was a reputed artist, musician, and experimental filmmaker long before she met John Lennon.

10 Ryuichi Sakamoto
Sakamoto (b. 1952), a prolific composer, wrote the music for Bertolucci's Oscar-winning film, *The Last Emperor*.

Left **Tokyo Metropolitan Museum of Photography** Right **A model on display, Edo-Tokyo Museum**

🔟 Museums

1 Edo-Tokyo Museum
This fabulous museum traces the history of Edo and Tokyo, charting its growth from a fishing village to today's megacity. Displays and models cover both the creation of the city and the natural and man-made disasters that have reshaped it *(see pp14–15)*.

2 ADMT Advertising Museum
The highly creative ad work on display at this extensive venue is sponsored by Dentsu, Japan's largest advertising operation. Exhibits cover the long history of commercial art in Japan. A TV room makes it possible to view commercials on demand *(see pp74–5)*.

3 Idemitsu Museum of Arts
Housing one of the finest private collections of Japanese and Asian art in Tokyo, this museum regularly rotates its exquisite Chinese, Korean, and Japanese ceramic ware and ancient pottery shards, calligraphy, and gold-painted screens *(see p73)*.

Urn, Idemitsu Museum of Arts

4 Japan Folk Crafts Museum
This museum displays a large collection of woodwork, ceramic ware, textiles, metal, glass work, and furniture created by largely unknown artists from Japan, China, Korea, and Taiwan. ⊗ *Map C2 • 4-3-33 Komaba, Meguro-ku • 3467-4527 • Open 10am–5pm Tue–Sun • Adm • www.mingeikan.or.jp*

5 Japanese Sword Museum
More than 30 of the 120 Japanese swords here are designated National Treasures, arguably the finest instruments of death ever made. A sword society was set up in 1948 during the US Occupation years, when swords were confiscated as a means of protecting the art of sword making. ⊗ *Map A4 • 4-25-10 Yoyogi, Shibuya-ku • 3379-1386 • Open 9am–4:30pm Tue–Sun • Adm*

6 Mori Art Museum
This museum focuses on art in a strongly cultural context, from video work, installation art, architecture, Japanese

Interior, ADMT Advertising Museum

➡ *Japan Folk Crafts Museum is set in the beautiful, prewar home of folk-art activist Yanagi Soetsu.*

conceptual, and pop, to retrospectives of British art. The shows, often radically different and sometimes contentious, change regularly. ◈ Map C6 • Mori Tower 52F–53F, 6-10-1 Roppongi, Minato-ku • 6406-6100 • Adm • www.mori.art. museum/html/eng/index

7 Tokyo Metropolitan Museum of Photography

The big names in Japanese and Western photography are shown at this premier photography and video art space in the city. Five floors follow the history of photography, displaying 23,000 images and photo-related items. Special exhibitions, featuring some of the world's best photographic work, run through the year. ◈ Map F1 • Ebisu Garden Place, 1-13-3 Mita, Meguro-ku • 3280-0099 • Open 10am–6pm Tue–Sun • Adm (only for special shows) • www.syabi.com

8 Tokyo National Museum

This large museum offers the world's largest collection of Japanese art and antiquity. Permanent Japanese exhibits are displayed in the Honkan; archeological relics in the Heiseikan Gallery; Chinese, Korean, and

Heiseikan Gallery, Tokyo National Museum

Central Asian arts in the Toyokan Gallery; and Buddhist sculpture and scrolls in the Gallery of Horyu-ji Treasures (see pp18–21).

9 Toguri Museum of Art

Featuring more than 7,000 works of fine Oriental porcelain, this museum rotates its collection seasonally. A small but lovely garden adds to the illusion of being far from busy Shibuya (see p96).

10 Ukiyo-e Ota Memorial Museum of Art

The museum's extensive private collection of ukiyo-e woodblock prints is constantly displayed in new showings. The images present a colorful cross-section of life in the city of Edo, from its streets and fish markets to the pleasure quarters (see p95).

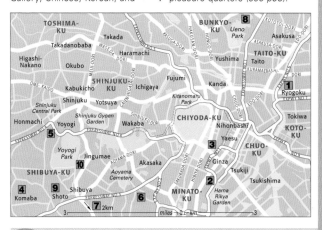

Recommend your favorite museum on traveldk.com

Left **Nikolai Cathedral** Center **Stone name plates, Nezu Shrine** Right **Gokoku-ji Temple**

TOP 10 Places of Worship

1 Sengaku-ji Temple

The graves of the 47 loyal *ronin* (retainers), who committed suicide after avenging their master's death *(see p32)*, are still visited by those who continue to honor their memory. The original temple dates from 1612. The main hall was obliterated in the 1945 air raids, but the reconstruction is faithful to the last detail *(see p110)*.

2 Gokoku-ji Temple

Statue of Confucius, Yushima Seido Temple

A rare find in modern Tokyo, this designated Important Cultural Treasure was built by the fifth shogun, Tsunayoshi, in 1681. The temple and the main gate have remained intact. Some interesting outbuildings include a wooden belfry and an ancient two-story pagoda. Despite its historical credentials, the temple grounds are little visited today.
⊗ *Map C1 • 5-40-1 Otsuka, Bunkyo-ku • 3941-0764*

3 Senso-ji Temple

This massive religious edifice, reconstructed after WWII, is the focus of life in the Asakusa district. The sweeping roof of the main hall is visible from the Kaminari-mon, the great gate to the temple. Inside the main hall, burning candles, incense sticks, and votive plaques add to the air of sanctity *(see pp10–11)*.

4 Hie Shrine

Reconstructed in 1967 after the Tokyo air raids, the 1659 building originally served as the protective shrine of Edo Castle. In gratitude, successive shoguns donated lavish gifts of swords and sacred horses to the shrine. A line of orange *torii* gates forms a colorful tunnel through the grounds *(see p90)*.

5 Yushima Seido Temple

One of the few Confucian temples in Tokyo, Yushima Seido was founded in 1632. The current site and its great stone-flagged courtyard date from 1935. A statue of Confucius is located near the main gate.
⊗ *Map F3 • 1-4-25 Yushima, Bunkyo-ku • 3251-4606 • Open 9:30am–5pm*

6 Kanda Myojin Shrine

A concrete reconstruction of the 1616 master design, this shrine has a green, oxidized roof,

Ornate gate, Kanda Myojin Shrine

⊖ *The Kanda Myojin Shrine is dedicated to the popular rebel Taira no Masakado.*

copper *torii* gate, and an ornate main entrance gate. ◈ *Map F3 • 2-16-2 Sotokanda, Chiyoda-ku • 3254-0753*

7 Yasukuni Shrine

Politics and religion coexist uncomfortably at Yasukuni Shrine, dedicated to the souls of Japan's war dead. Built in 1869, the shrine has some interesting features though, including an imposing *torii* gate, cherry trees, a pond garden, and teahouse. ◈ *Map D3 • 3-1-1 Kudankita, Chiyoda-ku • 3261-8326 • Open 6am–5pm*

8 Nezu Shrine

Established in 1706 by the fifth shogun, Tsunayoshi, Nezu Shrine is dedicated to Inari, the goddess of rice. The shrine grounds have retained most of the original structures. Tall cedars, gingko trees, and a carp pond create a strikingly natural setting. A painted gate, orange *torii* gates, and bright banners add color. ◈ *Map E1 • 1-28-9 Nezu, Bunkyo-ku • 3822-0753*

9 Meiji Shrine

Dedicated to the souls of the Meiji Emperor and his wife, this shrine was built in the pure

Gate to the Meiji Shrine, set amid greenery

Shinto architectural style. This is reflected in everything from its gravel forecourt, cypress pillars, and clean lines of the main hall to the copper roof that floats majestically above it all *(see pp24–5)*.

10 Nikolai Cathedral

Built with funds provided by a Russian czar and designed by English architect Josiah Conder, this late 19th-century Russian Orthodox church is an interesting anomaly among the temples and shrines of the city. It was named after its founder St. Nikolai Kassatkin, a 19th-century missionary who converted thousands of Japanese in the northern island of Hokkaido. ◈ *Map F3 • 4-1 Kanda-Surugadai, Chiyoda-ku • 3291-1885 • Open 1–3:30pm Tue–Fri*

[Map of central Tokyo showing numbered locations across wards including BUNKYO-KU, TAITO-KU, SHINJUKU-KU, CHIYODA-KU, CHUO-KU, KOTO-KU, and SHIBUYA-KU. Locations labeled: Takada, Takadanobaba, Haramachi, Okubo, Kabukicho, Shinjuku, Yotsuya, Yoyogi, Sendagaya, Jingumae, Akasaka, Wakaba, Kitanomaru Park, Ichigaya, Fujimi, Yushima, Ueno, Ueno Park, Matsugaya, Asakusa, Yanagibashi, Kanda, Nihonbashi, Imperial Palace Plaza, Yaesu, Ginza, Hibiya, Shinkawa, Tsukiji, Ryogoku, Tokiwa, Saga, Koishikawa Botanical Garden, Shinjuku Gyoen Garden, Yoyogi Park]

The Yasukuni Shrine hosts outdoor performances of traditional music, dance, and sumo wrestling.

Left **Interior, Spiral** Right **A display at Gallery Ma**

TOP 10 Art Galleries

1 21_21 Design Sight
Issey Miyake's work inspired the design of this superb building, created by architect Ando Tadao. The gallery-cum-studio also operates as a research center and workshop, bringing together artists, craftspeople, and designers with companies and consumers. ⊗ *Map C6 • 9-7-6 Akasaka, Minato-ku • 3475-2121 • Open 11am–8pm Tue–Sun • Adm • www.2121designsight.jp*

2 Spiral
Designed by leading architect Fumihiko Maki, this multipurpose gallery presents art, music, film, and theater. A spiral ramp curves above an elegant first-floor café, leading visitors into the main gallery spaces *(see p95)*.

3 Pentax Forum
Exhibitions of Japanese and world photography – from monochrome documentary to digitized semi-graphic work – is shown in this eclectic gallery.

People interested in the hardware will have great fun picking up and testing all the equipment on display *(see p103)*.

4 P3 – Art and Environment
Devoted to exploring the environment through art, this gallery holds exhibitions of video art, sound installations, and documentary work. Past shows have included the series "Project for Humankind" and "Project for Extraterrestrials." ⊗ *Map C3 • Tocho-ji Temple, B1, 4-34 Yotsuya, Shinjuku-ku • 3353-6866 • Open 10am–6pm*

5 The Tolman Collection
This gallery has 2,000-plus contemporary Japanese prints, aquatints, etchings, lithographs, and woodblocks. Signed and numbered editions of work by artists such as Araki Shinko and Gojo Miki are also included. ⊗ *Map E6 • 2-2-18 Shiba Daimon, Minato-ku • 3434-1300 • Open 11am–7pm Wed–Mon • www.tolmantokyo.com*

Paintings displayed in Pentax Forum

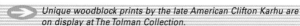
Unique woodblock prints by the late American Clifton Karhu are on display at The Tolman Collection.

6 INAX Gallery

Run by Inax Corp., makers of ceramic products, sanitary ware and tiles, this eclectic design gallery highlights media as varied as ceramic ware and video installation work. Two galleries are located on the second floor, focusing on architecture, design, and contemporary art forms *(see p76)*.

INAX Gallery, exterior

7 SCAI – The Bathhouse

This gallery is located in a converted Edo-period bathhouse in the endearingly old district of Yanaka. It showcases well-known experimental Japanese artists, in addition to helping to introduce foreign artists to Japan. ◈ *Map F1 • Kashiwaya-Ato, 6-1-23 Yanaka, Taito-ku • 3821-1144 • Open noon–7pm Tue–Sat • www.scaithebathhouse.com*

8 Gallery Ma

The bathroom appliance maker Toto set up Gallery Ma as a prime venue for modern architecture, one of the most comprehensive spaces of its kind. Recent exhibitions have showcased the sustainable designs of Glenn Murcatt, the latest work of Chinese architect Yung Ho Chang, and the earthquake-proof domes of Spaniard Felix Candela. ◈ *Map C6 • 3F, 1-24-3 Minami-Aoyama, Minato-ku • 3402-1010 • Open 11am–6pm Tue–Thu, 11am–7pm Fri • www.toto.co.jp/gallerma*

9 Tokyo Wonder Site

A Tokyo Metropolitan Government-run operation, Tokyo Wonder Site aims to promote new, emerging artists. With exhibitions on its three floors turning over at a rapid pace, this gallery represents a busy art environment. ◈ *Map A6 • 1-19-8 Jinnan, Shibuya-ku • 3463-0606 • Open 11am–7pm Tue–Sun • www.tokyo-ws.org/english/shibuya/index.html*

10 Zeit-Foto Salon

This is one of the oldest photo galleries in Tokyo, with a huge collection of images that encompasses 19th-century prints and the work of masters in the order of Man Ray and Lee Friedlander. Controversial Japanese artists, including photographer Ryoko Suzuki, and big international names ensure that the shows are always stimulating. ◈ *Map P2 • Matsumoto Bldg, 4F, 1-10-5 Kyobashi, Chuo-ku • 3535-7112 • Open 10:30am–6:30pm Tue–Fri, 10:30am–5:30pm Sat • www.zeit-foto.com*

Left **Asakusa Imahan** Center **Yoshiba** Right **Bird Land**

Restaurants

Asakusa Imahan

This early exponent of beef dishes opened its first restaurant in 1895. The specialty here is *shabu-shabu*, wafer-thin slices of prime beef cooked at your table in a pot of boiling water and served with seasonal vegetables. The seating here is at low tables on *tatami* mats *(see p87)*.

Sushi Ouchi

At this sushi haven, Chef Hisashi Ouchi uses only natural ingredients and eschews MSG, chemical additives, and coloring. Even the soy sauce, vinegar, *miso* soup, and green tea that go with yellowtail, tuna, or conger eel, are organic. ◎ Map A6 • 2-8-4 Shibuya, Shibuya-ku • 3407-3543 • Open noon–1:30pm, 5–11:30pm • ¥¥¥

A sushi platter at Sushi Ouchi

Yoshiba

Chankonabe, a robust stew of chicken, fish, and vegetables – the staple diet of sumo wrestlers – is the main dish served here.

You are likely to see wrestlers from one of the nearby sumo stables at the next table. ◎ Map H3 • 2-14-5 Yokoammi, Sumida-ku • 3623-4480 • Open 5–11pm Tue–Sat • ¥¥

Bird Land

The fame of this grill rests on its high-quality *yakitori*, sticks of charcoal-broiled chicken doused in a slightly sweet soy-based sauce. The chicken cuts here are closer to the lighter Chinese kebobs than the Turkish or Central Asian varieties. The smoky meat goes well with Japanese draft beer *(see p79)*.

Kanda Yabu Soba

This venerable restaurant serves classic Edo-period, hand-made *soba* (buckwheat noodles) along with some simple vege-table and pickle side dishes. The old wooden building creates a timeless mood. ◎ Map F3 • 2-10 Kanda-Awajicho, Chiyoda-ku • 3251-0287 • Open 11:30am–8pm • ¥¥¥

A busy day at Kanda Yabu Soba

Hantei

Hantei specializes in very delectable *kushi-age*, deep-fried skewers of meat, fish, and vegetables served with small side dishes. Items are served six at a time, and the menu is set, dispensing with the need to consult the English menu *(see p87)*.

Hantei restaurant interior

Kisso

Kaiseki, Japan's haute cuisine, can be expensive. An exquisitely prepared, multicourse eating experience, it features dishes prepared with fresh ingredients, many of which are seasonal. Kisso's mini-*kaiseki* lunch sets, served in beautifully crafted lacquerware alongside simple flower arrangements, are a great affordable option. ⊗ *Map D6 • B1, 5-17-1 Roppongi, Minato-ku • 3582-4191 • Open 11am–2pm, 5:30–9pm Mon–Sat • ¥–¥¥ (lunch), ¥¥¥ (dinner)*

Sasanoyuki

Many Tokyoites consider Sasanoyuki to be the city's finest tofu restaurant. It has an illustrious history, with connections to the imperial family and the high abbot at Kanei-ji Temple during the Edo period, when the restaurant opened. The atmosphere is relaxed and the service unfussy *(see p87)*.

Maisen

The Maisen chain is famous for its delicious *tonkatsu* (deep-fried pork cutlets), served with rice, a bed of shredded cabbage, and miso soup. Cutlets can be dipped in their own brand of sauce. Alternatives to meat are delicately fried shrimp and oysters served with a dribble of lemon. This Maisen branch is located in a converted bathhouse *(see p99)*.

Ten-Ichi Deux

More like a casual modern café than a restaurant, Ten-Ichi Deux serves tempura sets in the lighter Kyoto style. The seafood and vegetable sets, served with light side dishes, are manageable. Another good option is the simple *tendon*, deep-fried shrimp served on a bed of rice *(see p78)*.

Left **Interior, Sasagin** Right **Matcha** tea in a traditional tea bowl

Cafés and Bars

1 Kamiya Bar
The oldest Western-style bar in town, this Tokyo institution was established in 1880. The bar was set up by Kamiya Denbei, who also built Japan's first brandy distillery. Once favored by writers and artists, the bar still serves its signature *denki-bran*, a cocktail made with cognac, gin, and wine. ◈ *Map R2 • 1-1-1 Asakusa, Taito-ku • 3841-5400 • Open 11:30am–10pm Wed–Mon*

2 Pure Café
Organic coffee makes a good start to the day at this vegetarian, vegan, and macrobiotic café. Also on the menu are Chinese medicinal teas, beer, and wine. A self-service café serves light sandwiches, soups, grain sets, and cakes. ◈ *Map C6 • 5-5-21 Minami-Aoyama, Minato-ku • 5466-2611 • Open 8:30am–10:30pm*

3 Quons
The indoor bar at this stylish establishment features plush divans and leather chairs, while the bohemian roof terrace sports faux-Balinese furnishings. If the house champagne is a little steep, try the more affordable French and Argentinian wines, or one of their original cocktails. The food menu has an Asian accent. ◈ *Map B6 • 2F, 5-51-6 Jingumae, Shibuya-ku • 5468-0633 • Open 6pm–5am Mon–Sat, 6pm–2am Sun*

4 Awamori
Awamori is a fiery Okinawan alcohol distilled from Thai rice. This bar of the same name has an impressive 150 *awamori*, which the staff can help you choose from. Best served on the rocks and, if possible, with a slice of Okinawan lime. ◈ *Map N5 • 7-17-18 Higashi-Ginza, Chuo-ku • 3543-9256 • Open 5:30–11:30pm Mon–Sat*

5 Paddy Foley's Irish Pub
This long-established Irish pub offers an impressive range of beers and stouts, though draft Guinness draws the crowds. The food menu includes chicken and squid, besides the usual fish and chips and shepherds' pie offerings. ◈ *Map D6 • Roi Bldg, B1F, 5-5-1 Roppongi, Minato-ku • 3423-2250 • Open 5pm–1am*

Bar counter at Paddy Foley's Irish Pub

6 Sasagin
A great place to sample different types of Japanese sake. Tastes range from the syrupy sweet to the highly rated acerbically dry. Top-grade

Note that awamori, a deceptively simple drink to ease into, ranges from a 25 percent alcohol content to double that.

sake, such as the divine *dai ginjo*, is usually served chilled. ◈ *Map A5 • 1-32-15 Yoyogi-Uehara, Shibuya-ku • 5454-3715 • Open 5–11pm Mon–Sat*

7 Café Paulista

One of Tokyo's oldest. The coffee beans

The 52nd-floor Mado Lounge bar

here are the very best Brazilian, so the brews are strong and aromatic. For a prime location, the prices are surprisingly low. ◈ *Map M5 • Nagasaki Center, 8-9-16 Ginza, Chuo-ku • 3572-6160 • Open 8:30am–10pm Mon–Sat, noon–8pm Sun*

8 Cha Ginza

A shortened version of the Japanese tea ceremony here includes whisking the creamy brew into a bubbly froth and serving it with a Japanese sweet. The second floor serves *sancha* (ordinary green leaf tea). ◈ *Map M4 • 2-3F, 5-5-6 Ginza, Chuo-ku • 3571-1211 • Open 11am–7pm Tue–Mon*

9 Mado Lounge

The interior of this 52nd-floor bar consists of reflective wall and ceiling surfaces that

create a shimmering effect. Upholstered couches give way to simple furniture ranged along the viewing area, which is equipped with the main service bar and a control center for mellow sounds and visuals. ◈ *Map C6 • Mori Tower 52F, 6-10-1 Roppongi, Minato-ku • 6406-6652 • Open 10am–11pm Mon–Thu, 10am–midnight Fri–Sat*

10 Ben's Café

Students from nearby Waseda University and arty expatriates favor this American-style café. The coffee is excellent, the cakes and homemade bagels tasty. A good range of Japanese and imported German beers is also available. ◈ *Map B3 • 1-29-21 Takadanobaba, Shinjuku-ku • 3202-2445 • Open 11:30am–11:30pm Mon–Thu, 11:30–12:30am Fri–Sat*

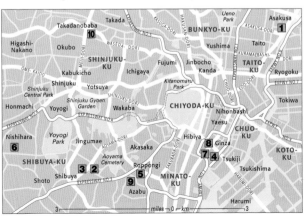

Left **Takeshita-dori** Center **Shibuya Beam** Right **Tokyo Anime Center**

🔟 Pop Culture Venues

1 Tokyo Big Sight
Arguably Asia's largest art festival, the biannual, two-day Design Festa *(see p56)* is held at the Tokyo Big Sight. ⬡ *Map D2* • *Tokyo International Exhibition Centre, 3-21-2 Ariake, Koto-key* • *5530-1111* • *Adm*

2 Takeshita-dori
Packed with garish boutiques, subculture junk, cutesy accessories, lurid kitsch, and fetish costumery, this loud, abrasive, fun street is preferred by Japanese extreme youth. ⬡ *Map B5* • *Takeshita-dori, Shibuya-ku*

3 Center Gai
A bustling pedestrian street crammed with inexpensive bars, cafés, and restaurants, as well as stores selling a wide range of music records, cell phones, clothes, and jewelry, Center Gai is the epicenter of Japanese youth culture. Full of teens and early-20s. ⬡ *Map R5* • *Shibuya, Shibuya-ku*

Shoppers thronging neon-lit Center Gai

4 Pokémon Center
Children can follow the adventures of familiar TV anime and film characters, such as Pikachu and Ash Ketchum, as they travel to Cerulean City or the Orange Islands. ⬡ *Map E6* • *2F, Shiba-Rikyu Bldg, 1-2-3 Shiodome, Minato-ku* • *6430-7733* • *Open noon–8pm*

5 Manga no Mori
This store boasts a terrific range of Japanese manga and anime, with a small showing of imported comics featuring superheroes, cute characters, and bondage. *Doujinsha*, a subculture level of manga, is produced by gifted fans and amateurs. ⬡ *Map R5* • *12-10 Udagawa-cho, Shibuya-ku* • *5489-0257* • *Open 10am–10pm*

6 Shibuya Beam
Beam hosts live game spots, comedy duos, interviews, and anime-inspired *cosplay* shows. The first floor has a Namco game arcade. Repair upstairs to the J-Pop Café for coffee and music. ⬡ *Map Q5* • *B2F, 31-2 Udagawa, Shibuya-ku* • *3477-0777*

7 Sunday in the Park
Tokyo's theater of dress spills over from busy Harajuku into Yoyogi Park every Sunday, where you may chance upon costumes reflecting every trend since the 1950s. Live bands set up

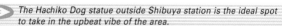

The Hachiko Dog statue outside Shibuya station is the ideal spot to take in the upbeat vibe of the area.

Youth in Goth attire, Harajuku

during the afternoon along the sidewalk between the park and Olympic pavilions (see p47).

8 Hachiko Crossing
A battery of neon and liquid crystal transmits endless streams of commercial messaging and colors across the buildings in this fashion town. The central panel, Q-Front, is the largest video screen in Tokyo. ◈ *Map A4–6, B4–6 • Shibuya station north exit, Shibuya-ku*

9 Tokyo Anime Center
Japan's largest anime center is devoted to promoting anime films, games, and character products. Its digital theater and dubbing studio stage 200 annual live events involving voice actors and anime creators. ◈ *Map F3 • 4F, UDX Bldg, 4-14-1 Soto-Kanda, Chiyoda-ku • 5298-1188 • Open 11am–7pm*

10 Comiket
The three-day-long Comiket (Comic Market) trade fair is the mecca for manga fans. Hundreds of booths display and sell a bewildering range of items, from old Atom Boy comics and the Neon Genesis Evangelion series to the Tekkonkinkret comic and anime creation. ◈ *Map D2 • Tokyo Big Sight, 3-21-2 Ariake, Koto-ku • 5530-1111 • Open late Dec/mid-Aug: 10am–4pm*

Top 10 Cultural Phenomena

1 Hello Kitty
Launched in 1974, this helplessly naive but adorable creature has a button nose and, inexplicably, no mouth.

2 Cosplay
Cosu-pure, or costume play, refers to cross-dressing in outfits worn by manga or anime characters.

3 Capsule Hotels
Architect Kurokawa Kisho's 1970 Nakagin Capsule Building inspired the idea of the capsule hotel.

4 Maid Cafés
Young women in white tights, pink hair, lace caps, and aprons respectfully serve tea and cakes.

5 Akihabara
The world's largest electronic goods center also attracts manga and anime followers to its *cosplay* shows.

6 Manga Kissa
For a cup of coffee at a *kissa*, short for *kissaten* (café), manga fans can access hundreds of comic books.

7 Hip Fashion Minorities
Harajuku and Shibuya are full of cyber-punks and "Goth-Loli" – girls in black makeup and Victorian frills.

8 Otaku
Otaku – geeks or nerds – are passionate about anime, manga, video games, and cute female star merchandise.

9 Love Hotels
There are over 20,000 love hotels in Tokyo alone, featuring various fantasy themes.

10 Pachinko
Pachinko, or Japanese pinball, is considered low-brow, but there are parlors on almost every shopping street.

Left **Yoyogi Park** Center **Shinjuku Gyoen Garden** Right **Koishikawa Korakuen Garden**

🏵10 Gardens and Parks

1 Canadian Embassy Garden

Built across an upper terrace of the building, this stone garden was created by Masuno Shunmyo, one of the most innovative garden designers working in Japan today. The stone garden symbolizes, through the use of stones brought from Hiroshima to represent the ancient rocks that form the Canadian Shield, the relationship between Japan and Canada. ◈ *Map C5 • Canadian Embassy, 4F, 7-3-38 Akasaka, Minato-ku • 3408-2101 • Open 9:30am–5pm Mon–Sat*

2 Hibiya Park

Part of a feudal estate converted into a military parade ground, Hibiya Park was Japan's first Western-style park when it opened in 1903. A lawn, rose garden, bandstand, and theater occupy the center of the park. A pond, with its original fountain in the shape of a heron, and a giant wisteria trellis are tucked away in the western corner. *(see p74).*

3 Koishikawa Korakuen Garden

Tokyo's oldest garden, Koishikawa Korakuen was laid out in 1629, re-creating famous scenes in miniature from Japan and China. It was commissioned by Tokugawa Yorifusa, founder of the Mito clan. A simple grass-covered knoll represents Mount Lu in China's Jiangxi Province, while a shallow stream stands in for Oikawa River in Kyoto *(see pp22–3).*

4 Mukojima Hyakka-en Garden

This little-visited Edo-period garden was completed in 1804 close to Sumida River *(see pp12–13)*, a district of temples and teahouses serving as the focal point for a refined social and cultural life. ◈ *Map D1 • 3-18-3 Mukojima, Sumida-ku • 3611-8705 • Open 9am–5pm • Adm*

5 Kiyosumi-teien Garden

Rare rocks were shipped from all over the country in steam ships to create this garden, which was once part of an estate owned by a rich timber merchant. A traditional teahouse overlooks a large pond and islets. Another eye-catching feature of this garden is an artificial hill, shaped into the likeness of Mount Fuji. ◈ *Map H4 • Kiyosumi 3-3-9, Koto-ku • 3641-5892 • Open 9am–5pm • Adm*

Visitors inside Kiyosumi-teien Garden

6 Nature Study Institute and Park

A carefully preserved section of the Musashino Plain, this park is home to a variety of birds, insects, and turtles, in addition to 8,000-plus trees. A small museum at the entrance traces Tokyo's declining greenery. ◉ *Map C2 • 5-21-5 Shirokanedai, Minato-ku • 3441-7176 • Open May–Aug: 9am–5pm Tue–Sun; Sep–Apr: 9am–4:30pm • Adm*

Teahouse with azaleas in bloom, Hama Rikyu Garden

7 Rikugi-en Garden

Completed in 1702, this garden was named after the six principles used in the composition of Oriental poetry. While the garden's hidden symbolism is not easy to decipher, its curvaceous landscapes, simple Zen-style teahouses, and profusion of trees can be appreciated by all. ◉ *Map D1 • 6-16-3 Honkomagome, Bunkyo-ku • 3941-2222 • Open 9am–5pm • Adm*

8 Shinjuku Gyoen Garden

Excelling at variety, Shinjuku Gyoen Garden was completed in 1772. The current garden, a multicultural masterpiece, is divided into French, English, and Japanese sections. An old, domed botanical greenhouse houses tropical plants. The garden is also a popular spot for cherry blossom viewing in the spring *(see p104)*.

9 Hama Rikyu Garden

An original Edo-period garden, Hama Rikyu dates from 1654. Standing near the garden entrance is a large black pine, planted in 1704, a miraculous survivor

of earthquakes, fires, and air raids. The most unique feature of this large garden is a tidal pond that brings in salt-water fish *(see p75)*.

10 Yoyogi Park

A wide open area of grassy lawns and recreational facilities popular with families, bicyclists, joggers, and skateboarders, Yoyogi Park makes a great spot for an impromptu picnic. A small botanical garden and bird sanctuary add interest and live music concerts are held here every Sunday *(see p44)*. The park forms one of the largest forested areas of Tokyo. ◉ *Map A5 • 1 Yoyogi-Kamizono-cho, Shibuya-ku • 3469-6081 • Open all day*

Left **Ministry of Justice Building** Center **Nikolai Cathedral** Right **Hattori Building**

🔟 Historic Buildings

Bank of Japan
The bank's solid Neoclassical outline was designed by Tatsuno Kingo, Japan's first Western-style architect. The 1896 building stands on the old site of the shogunate's former mints. A guided tour in English introduces the structure, as well as its history and present-day function *(see p68)*.

Crafts Gallery
The finely finished, Meiji-era structure, which houses the Crafts Gallery, originally served as the headquarters of the Imperial Guard. Built in a style that came to be known as "19th-century Renaissance," it is one of the few protected buildings in a city notorious for its weak preservation ethic *(see p67)*.

Kyu Iwasaki-tei Mansion
A fine example of Meiji-era syncreticism, this grand 1896 wooden residence was built by English architect Josiah Conder in a mix of Jacobean, Gothic, and

Imposing façade of Kyu Iwasaki-tei Mansion

Pennsylvanian country styles. Original features include coffered wood ceilings, stone fireplaces, parquet flooring, and Japan's first Western-style toilet. 🔍 *Map F2*
• *1-3-45 Ikenohata, Taito-ku* • *3823-8033*
• *Open 9am–5pm* • *Adm*

Buddha statue, Gokoku-ji Temple

Gokoku-ji Temple
The temple grounds have some interesting features, including a belfry and a rare two-story pagoda. The main hall, with its colossal wooden pillars, massive copper roof, and dark interior full of priceless Buddhist artifacts, is the centerpiece of this grand complex *(see p36)*.

Hattori Building
The 1932 structure, created by Watanabe Hitoshi, is a Ginza landmark. It is also known as the Wako Building, after the jewelers it houses. With its curving frontage and clock tower, the building appears as a backdrop in several old movies. The grand interior is as impressive. 🔍 *Map M4* • *4-5-11 Ginza, Chuo-ku* • *3562-2111* • *Open 10:30am–6pm*

Hongan-ji Temple
Even in a city known for its architectural hybrids, this temple, strongly suggestive of Indian architecture, is an extraordinary one. Its designer, Ito Chuta, traveled all over Asia and this is reflected in his 1935 building, where he pays homage to the

Hongan-ji Temple, a tribute to the Indian roots of Japanese Buddhism

Indian origins of Japanese Buddhism. ⊗ Map N5 • 3-15-1 Tsukiji, Chuo-ku • 3541-1131

7 Kudan Kaikan

Part Western, but with a temple-like roof, the Kudan Kaikan is a mélange of architectural styles. Like many Japanese buildings created in the 1930s, it reflects a yearning to return to a more traditional national style of architecture, with a lingering fondness for Western styles, such as Art Deco. ⊗ Map L1 • 1-6-5 Kudan-minami, Chiyoda-ku • 3261-5521

8 Ministry of Justice Building

Although this building is not open to the public, its exterior, well-renovated in the 1990s, is worth a look. A German company, Ende and Bockman, designed this 1895 redbrick structure in a style that mixes formal elegance with functionality. ⊗ Map L4 • 1-1-1 Kasumigaseki, Chiyoda-ku • 3580-4111

9 Nikolai Cathedral

The 1891 cathedral was lucky to survive the 1923 earthquake, with only its onion domes destroyed. A new green dome was placed on top of the cruciform Russian Orthodox church after the disaster, and impressive stained-glass windows were installed (see p37).

10 Tokyo Station

Threatened with demolition on many occasions, the Tokyo Station building has survived due to the relentless efforts of preservation groups over the years. Its future now seems assured. Designed by Tatsuno Kingo, the 1914 structure is faced with locally made bricks and reinforced with steel shipped from Britain and the United States (see p67).

Left **Kiddyland** Right **Tomioka Hachimangu Flea Market**

🔟 Stores and Markets

1 Fuji Torii
In business since the 1950s, Fuji Tori stocks a good range of high-quality Imari porcelain, woodblock prints, scrolls, Buddhist statuary, *tansu* chests, and lacquerware. The products sold here are priced fairly and their authenticity is certified. Hand-painted screens are its specialty. The English-speaking staff are friendly and willing to help customers. ◈ *Map S4 • 6-1-10 Jingumae, Shibuya-ku • 3400-2777 • Open 11am–6pm Wed–Mon*

2 Laox
Close to the station, Laox is located in the heart of "Electric Town" Akihabara, the world's largest electrical goods district. Japan's biggest supplier of electronic goods, the store sells items and accessories that are adapted for overseas use. Laox also supplies manuals and catalogs in English and other languages. ◈ *Map F3 • 1-15-3 Soto-Kanda, Chiyoda-ku • 3253-7111 • Open 10am–9pm*

3 Akebono
This store specializes in *wagashi*, traditional Japanese sweets, which are like petite cakes made from rice, bean paste, and sweet potato. A delight for the eyes as much as the palate, *wagashi* are served during the tea ceremony. Akebono's sweets are sold in some of the better department store food basements *(see p77)*.

4 Kinokuniya Bookstore
The sixth-floor selection of English books here is one of the best and largest in Tokyo. It offers a good number of books in French and German, and a wide variety of magazines in English. Kinokuniya also has a second, smaller store along nearby Shinjuku-dori. ◈ *Map B4 • Takashimaya Times Square, Sedagaya 3-17-7, Shinjuku-ku • 3354-0131 • Open 10am–8pm*

5 Ameyoko Market
From modest beginnings as a postwar black market specializing in sweets made from potato, Ameyoko has developed into an amazing street with over 500 stalls and small shops built under the JR railway tracks. A favorite spot for very fresh, pre-New Year food goods, especially fish. ◈ *Map F2 • Ueno Station • Timings vary*

Stores and stalls in Ameyoko Market

Tower Records

6 This Shibuya store has six floors of music to suit every taste. The seventh-floor bookstore stocks an extensive line in fiction, photography, travel, musical books, and a wide range of magazines and newspapers. ⊗ *Map R5 • 1-22-14 Jinnan, Shibuya-ku • 3496-3661 • Open 10am–10pm*

Tokyu Hands

7 Part hardware, home novelty, and DIY store, Tokyu Hands stocks just about everything for the interior, from sofas to electrically heated slippers, Swiss army knives, and a whole section devoted to party goods. ⊗ *Map R5 • 12-18 Udagawa-cho, Shibuya-ku • 5489-5111 • Open 10am–8:30pm*

Tomioka Hachimangu Flea Market

8 One of the best flea markets in Tokyo, in terms of choice, scale, and location. If the antique furniture is too expensive, take a look at the cheap ceramic ware, the boxes of old postcards, or the old kimono fabrics, a favorite with young people who design their own clothes. ⊗ *Map H5 • 1-20-3 Tomioka, Koto-ku • 3642-1315 • Open 1st & 2nd Sun of the month*

Striking exterior of Mikimoto Ginza 2

Mikimoto Ginza 2

9 This second Mikimoto store in the Ginza, designed by Ito Toyo, is certainly the most interesting one to look at from the outside. The store chain was named after Mikimoto Kokichi, who created the cultured pearl back in 1893 *(see p77)*.

Kiddyland

10 With six floors of toys, stationery, and sweets, this children's store is truly a kiddy heaven. Joining old character favorites, such as Hello Kitty, Godzilla, Ultraman, and Pokémon, are gadgets, games, and novelties. ⊗ *Map S4 • 6-1-9 Jingumae, Shibuya-ku • 3409-3431 • Open 10am–8pm*

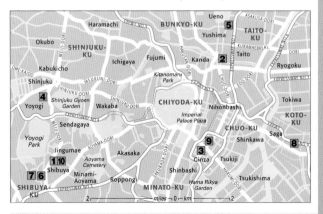

Left **Japan Traditional Craft Center** Center **Hara Shobo** Right **Sagemonoya**

🔟 Art and Craft Stores

1 Bingo-ya

In addition to Japanese traditional crafts, ranging from ceramics and glassware to fabrics and local crafts, the store also stocks overseas folk arts and crafts. ⓢ *Map C1 • 10-6 Wakamatsu-cho, Shinjuku-ku • 3202-8778 • Open 10am–7pm Tue–Sun*

2 Tsutsumo Factory

At Tsutsumo (meaning "to wrap") the specialty is wrapping paper. The finest, *washi*, is a thick, handmade variety that can also be used to make bags, small boxes, and hats. ⓢ *Map Q5 • 37-15 Udagawa-cho, Shibuya-ku • 5478-1330 • Open 10am–7pm Mon–Sat*

3 Kyukyodo

A well-established paper specialist, Kyukyodo first set up business in 1663, though its current location dates from 1880. It sells superior handmade *washi* paper, as well as gift cards, ornamental boxes, picture frames, and a superb range of incense *(see p77)*.

4 Blue & White

The emphasis here is on exquisitely crafted modern and traditional everyday items. The fans, textiles, porcelain, candles, and picture frames are in indigo-dyed blue

An array of textiles at Blue & White

and white. ⓢ *Map J6 • 2-9-2 Azabu-Juban, Minato-ku • 3451-0537 • Open 10am–6pm Mon–Sat*

5 Isetatsu

This venerable paper-craft store sells miniature chests made from *washi* paper and *chiyogami*, as well as designs of original samurai textiles produced from painstakingly carved wooden blocks. ⓢ *Map F1 • 2-18-9 Yanaka, Taito-ku • 3823-1453 • Open 10am–6pm*

6 Hara Shobo

Specializing in woodblock prints and illustrated books from the 17th century to *shin-hanga* (modern prints), Hara Shobo also sells original woodblock work at surprisingly affordable prices. The store has been in business since the 1880s. ⓢ *Map E3 • 2–3 Kanda-Jimbocho, Chiyoda-ku • 5212-7801 • Open 10am–6pm Tues-Sat*

Kyukyodo's imposing exterior

7 Japan Traditional Craft Center

The center was set up to promote an understanding of traditional Japanese crafts as well as the work of living artists. Some of the tools to craft the kiminos, dolls, lacquerware, and ceramics are for sale, too. ⊗ *Map C1 • Metropolitan Plaza, 1-2F, 1-11-1 Nishi Ikebukuro, Toshima-ku • 5954-6066 • Open 11am–7pm*

8 Japan Sword

This unique store has been in business since the Meiji period, when the samurai were superannuated and their martial equipment became collectable. Reproductions are also sold here. ⊗ *Map D6 • 3-8-1 Toranomon, Minato-ku • 3434-4321 • Open 9:30am–6pm Mon–Fri, 9:30am–5pm Sat*

9 Sagemonoya

The stunning range here includes Inro, Yatate, and pipecases, as well as superbly carved Netsuke – miniature ivory and wood sculptures. ⊗ *Map C3 • Palais Eternal Bldg, 702-703, 4-28-20 Yotsuya, Shinjuku-ku • 3352-6286 • Open 1:30–6pm Wed–Sat*

10 Oriental Bazaar

This is a great place to buy a wide array of gifts, including *yukata* (summer kimono) as well as original and reproduction woodblock prints. ⊗ *Map S4 • 5-9-13 Jingumae, Shibuya-ku • 3400-3933 • Open 10am–7pm Mon–Wed, Fri–Sun*

Guardian lions outside Oriental Bazaar

Top 10 Things to Buy

1 Ceramic Ware
Some of the big names to look out for are Mino, Arita, Raku, Bizen, and Mashiko.

2 Yukata
Yukata, light cotton kimonos worn during the humid summer months, are comfortable and portable.

3 Woodblock prints
Woodblock prints depict lovely women of the pleasure quarters, popular actors, and famous landscapes.

4 Hagoita
The *Hagoita* (Japanese shuttlecocks) are painted with the faces of kabuki actors, courtesans, and TV celebrities.

5 Bamboo
A very versatile wood, used to craft everything from chopsticks to window blinds and flower baskets.

6 Dolls
Originally used as talismans to ward off evil, dolls are now displayed in festivals and sold as toys and souvenirs.

7 Lacquerware
Good lacquerware can be expensive. Be warned that in dry air it will eventually crack.

8 Antiques
Antiques are found in both upmarket stores and flea markets. Kotto-dori in Aoyama is known as "antique street."

9 Handmade paper
Thick *washi* paper has many uses, including calligraphy, painting, making lanterns, umbrellas, and fans.

10 Incense
The finest and the most expensive incense comes from smokeless wood chips of trees that are naturally scented.

 Sagemonoya can be visited by appointment only. The staff here are fluent in English.

Left **Nature Study Institute and Park** Right **Lion Beer Hall**

⑩ Ways to Unwind

1 Green Tea at Rikugi-en

Set beautifully near Rikugi-en's large pond, with an immaculate lawn in front, Fukiage-no-chaya teahouse serves *matcha* powdered green tea and tiny Japanese sweets, similar to those at Takimi-no-chaya, a teahouse cantilevered over an inlet of the pond *(see p47)*.

Green Tea, Rikugi-en garden

2 Nature Study Institute and Park

This spacious, undeveloped track of nature is formed from an untouched section of the original Musashino Plain. This wonderland is home to 8,000 trees, shrubs, and flowers *(see p47)*.

3 Riverboat Cruises

Suijo water buses operate from the quay at Azuma Bridge in Asakusa, offering river cruises lasting up to 45 minutes, to the Hama-Rikyu Garden or onward to Odaiba Island. ◉ *Map R2 • 3457-7830 • www.suijobus.co.jp*

A *suijo* pleasure boat

4 Sun and Moon Yoga

Run by a Californian woman and her Japanese husband, both writers, the studio offers classes and workshops in breathing, meditation, and various styles of yoga. The Zen-like setting creates a soothing ambience. ◉ *Map C2 • Meguro Eki Mae Mansion, Higashi Guchi Building, Kami Osaki 3-1-5, Suite 204, Shinagawa-ku • 3280-6383*

5 Spa and Massage at The Four Seasons Hotel

The skin-care treatments here use products supplied exclusively to the Four Seasons Hotel: white lotus for relaxation, ginger flower for euphoria, rice for sensuality, and bamboo leaf for energy. These are applied in single or combined programs of body, face, scalp, and neck *(see p131)*.

6 Tower City View and Café

Tokyo City View observation deck offers sweeping vistas of the city. Head to the relaxing café or bar later. The tower's new 52nd-floor Sky Deck offers the chance to look down on the city from a ledge built around the rim of the rooftop heliport. ◉ *Map C6 • Mori Tower, 52F, 6-10-1 Roppongi, Minato-ku • 6406-6100*

Nezu Institute of Fine Arts Garden

Top 10 Hot Springs and Baths

1 Azabu-Juban Onsen
Here the water is a natural brown, with a lot of bucolic iron. ◈ Map D6 • 1-5-22 Azabu-Juban, Minato-ku • 3404-2610

2 Koshi-No-Yu-Sento
An authentic Japanese bathhouse, with Jacuzzi and sauna. ◈ Map D6 • 1-5-22 Azabu-Juban, Minato-ku • 3404-2610

3 Komparu-yu
Edo-period bathhouse with two tubs: atatakai (hot) and nurui (lukewarm). ◈ Map M5 • 8-7-5 Ginza, Chuo-ku • 3571-5469

4 Rokuryu Onsen
Traditional façade, huge interior with amber-colored water. ◈ Map F1 • 3-4-20 Ikenohata, Taito-ku • 3821-3826

5 Asakusa Kannon Public Baths
Historic bathhouse near Senso-ji Temple. ◈ Map R1 • 2-7-26 Asakusa, Taito-ku • 3844-4141

6 Jakotsu-Yu
Hot jet-powered brown waters followed by a cooler outdoor bath. ◈ Map R2 • 1-11-11 Asakusa, Taito-ku • 3841-8645

7 Oedo Onsen Monogatari
Hot-spring theme park, with multiple baths. ◈ Map D2 • 2-57 Aomi, Koto-ku • 5500-1126

8 Shimizu-yu
A traditional bathhouse. ◈ Map C6 • 3-12-3 Minami-Aoyama, Minato-ku • 3401-4404

9 La Qua Spa
The water here is great for poor circulation. ◈ Map E1 • La Qua Bldg, 6F, 1-1-1 Kasuga, Bunkyo-ku • 3817-4173

10 Seta Onsen
Indoor and outdoor baths in a garden setting. ◈ Map B2 • 4-15-30 Seta, Setagaya-ku • 3707-8228

7 Nezu Institute of Fine Arts Garden
This small but complex garden is a cross between a natural landscape and a tea garden. There are narrow paths, teahouses, an iris pond at the bottom of sloping hillsides, and Buddhist stone statuary (see p95).

8 Cocktails at the New York Bar
Cocktails at the Park Hyatt's New York Bar is Tokyo at its most urbane. The 52nd-floor daytime views take in distant Mount Fuji, while the nightscape resembles a brilliant, liquid-crystal forest (see p130).

9 Lion Beer Hall
Part of a 1930s building, this Bavarian-style beer hall is surprisingly down-to-earth and affordable for its location in upmarket Ginza. The pub menu, with variations on the theme of the sausage, makes for a good night out. ◈ Map M5 • 7-9-20 Ginza, Chuo-ku • 3571-2590

10 Nail Bee
Nail sculpturing, design, and coloring are hyper-fashionable in Tokyo. Besides a range of manicures and pedicures to make nails look like pop-art works, the salon offers eyelash and eyebrow treatments. ◈ Map N4 • Keitoku Bldg, 3F, 3-3-14 Ginza, Chuo-ku • 5250-0018 • Open 11am–8pm

 The Park Hyatt, home to the New York Bar, was the setting of the film Lost in Translation *(2003).*

Left **Design Festa display** Right **A procession on New Year's Day**

Festivals and Events

1 Design Festa
This biannual event, Asia's largest art festival, features 7,000 Japanese as well as international artists, musicians, and performers from every conceivable genre. Drawing over 50,000 visitors, the Design Festa also presents fashion shows, *cosplay* exhibitionists, and live bands. The two-day extravaganza of creativity is held at the Tokyo Big Sight *(see p44).* ✎ *May/Nov*

2 Coming-of-Age Day
The age of consent in Japan is 20, a milestone celebrated in Tokyo by visits to major shrines. The Meiji Shrine *(see pp24–5),* where an archery display is held to mark the event, is one of the most popular sites for adulthood ceremonies. ✎ *Map B5 • 1-1 Yoyogi-Kamizonocho, Shibuya-ku • 3379-5511*

3 Seven-Five-Three Festival
Children who have reached the ages of three, five, and seven, are dressed up in pint-sized traditional kimonos and taken to shrines to pray for their well-being at this delightful event. The numbers signify ages once considered milestones at a time when child mortality was high. The occasion is also a great photo opportunity. ✎ *Nov 15*

4 Kanda Matsuri
One of Tokyo's three major festivals, the Kanda Matsuri is held in odd-numbered years. It features sake, music, and dance, but the highlight is the more decorous Heian-period costume parade, a procession of floats, and *mikoshi* (portable shrines). ✎ *Map F3 • Kanda Myojin Shrine, Chiyoda-ku • 3254-0753 • Mid-May*

5 New Year's Day
Millions of Japanese pay homage to the New Year with visits to Shinto shrines and Buddhist temples throughout Tokyo. The most popular venues are the Meiji Shrine *(see pp24–5)* and Senso-ji Temple *(see pp10–11),* where bells are rung to welcome in the New Year. ✎ *Jan 1–4*

6 Sanja Festival
Tokyo's largest festival honors the two brothers who found a statue of Kannon, the Goddess of Mercy, in their nets. The spirits of the brothers and the shrine's deities are carried in portable shrines through the streets. ✎ *Map R1 • Senso-ji Temple, 2-3-1 Asakusa, Taito-ku • 3842-0181 • 3rd weekend of May*

7 Horseback Archery
Yabusame, or horseback archery, was integral to the samurai arts of war.

Girls at Seven-Five-Three Festival

A participant at the horseback archery

Men in samurai gear charge their mounts through Sumida Park, aiming to strike three targets in rapid succession.
🅢 Map S1 • Sumida Park, Taito-ku
• Mid-Apr

Sumida River Fireworks
As many as 1 million Tokyoites converge on the river-banks near Asakusa to see over 20,000 fireworks light up the skies and the Sumida River. The best viewing spots are from Komagata Bridge or between Shirahige and Kototoi bridges (see pp12–13). 🅢 Jul: last Sat

Tokyo Marathon
The Japanese take pride in their marathon runners, particu-larly women, who have won gold medals in past Olympics. Competing is a serious business, with very strict entrance rules and requirements. The run begins at the National Stadium, built for the 1964 Tokyo Olympics. 🅢 Map C4 • Mid-Feb

Water Purification Rites
Cleansing rituals are held at several shrines throughout Tokyo in winter. Young men and women, whose 20th birthdays fall in the same year, stand in pools full of blocks of ice and douse themselves with freezing buckets of water. 🅢 Map F3 • Kanda Myojin Shrine • Jan 10–12

Top 10 Flower and Plant Events

1 Plum Blossom Viewing
The blossoms at Yushima Tenjin Shrine attract Tokyoites.
🅢 Map F2 • Late Feb–early Mar

2 Cherry Blossom Viewing
Crowds picnic under the pink blossoms in parks and gardens. 🅢 Mid–late Apr

3 Peony Displays
Pink, red, and yellow peonies can be viewed at the Ueno Park's Tosho-gu Shrine.
🅢 Map F1 • Mid-April

4 Azalea Festival
Azaleas bloom at Nezu Shrine and the Imperial Palace East Gardens. 🅢 Map E1; L2, M2 • Apr 10–May 15 • Adm

5 Iris Viewing
Visit the iris gardens at the Meiji Shrine and Horikiri.
🅢 Map B5, D1 • Early–mid-Jun

6 Lotus Blossoms
Pink lotuses bloom in the Shinobazu Pond in Ueno Park.
🅢 Map F2 • Mid-Jul–Aug

7 Chinese Lantern Plant Fair
This popular fair is held in the Senso-ji Temple. 🅢 Map R1
• 3842-0181 • Jul 9–10

8 Morning Glory Fair
Vendors sell thousands of potted morning glories in the grounds of Kishimojin Temple.
🅢 Map C1 • Jul 6–8

9 Chrysanthemum Festival
Shinjuku Gyoen Garden has a wonderful exhibition of chrysanthemums. 🅢 Map B4, C4 • Late Oct–mid-Nov

10 Fall Leaves
Red maples, russet fall leaves, and yellow gingkos bloom in the parks and old Edo-period gardens.
🅢 Mid–late Nov

Lanterns, summer kimonos, watermelons, beer, and sake add to the festive occasion of the Sumida River Fireworks.

Left **Takarazuka Theater** Right **Asakusa Engei Hall**

⑩ Entertainment Venues

1 Cerulean Tower Noh Theater

Noh plays are almost abstract, but armed with an English script you can follow the stories of avenging spirits and wandering ghosts. The stage set at the Cerulean Tower Tokyu Hotel *(see p130)* presents sumptuous costumes, masks, sonorous music, and slow dance gestures. ◈ 3477-6412 (bookings)

Poster, Cerulean Tower Noh Theater

2 Aoyama Round Theater

One of Tokyo's few circular stages, this interestingly designed, midsize theater hosts contemporary dance shows, ballet, and musicals. Built within the National Children's Castle, it also presents programs for young audiences. Ticket prices at the 1,200-seat theater are reasonable. ◈ Map S5 • 5-31-1 Jingumae, Shibuya-ku • 3797-5678 • Open 10am–6pm

3 Takarazuka Theater

Established way back in 1914, the Takarazuka has been staging sentimental and romantic plays featuring exclusively female actors, unlike Kabuki, which is an all-male preserve. *The Rose of Versailles*, with its opulent costumes and dashing heroes, is a perennial favorite. Synopsis are provided in English. ◈ Map M4 • 1-1-3 Yurakucho, Chiyoda-ku • 5251-2001

4 Kanze Noh Theater

Kanze Noh-Gakudo, the troupe that performs here, is regarded as one of the finest in Tokyo. The spectacular dramas are staged in the open air by masked actors whose movements are lit up by massive burning torches. ◈ Map Q5 • 1-16-4 Shoto, Shibuya-ku • 3469-5241

5 Shimbashi Embujo

This theater stages period dramas, whose plots are strong on the conflict between love and duty. "Super-Kabuki," a modern dramatic form devised by veteran actor Ichikawa Ennosuke, guarantees to keep even non-Japanese audience members alert. ◈ Map N5 • 6-18-2 Ginza, Chuo-ku • 3541-2600

6 Asakusa Engei Hall

Traditional comic storytelling, *Rakugo*, takes place here. The seated narrators perform alone, with the barest of props, usually just a fan. Although it is exceedingly difficult for foreigners to follow, it is worth a visit for the atmosphere alone. ◈ Map G2 • 1-43-12 Asakusa, Taito-ku • 3841-8126

7 Azabu Die Pratze

Strictly for adults with leanings toward radical, innovative dance, this theater favors modern, occasionally

 Shimbashi Embujo puts on "Super-Kabuki" theatrical extravaganzas in April and May.

controversial dance dramas.
🔻 *Map D6 • 2-12 Nishi-Gokencho, Shinjuku-ku • 3235-7990*

8 New National Theater
Each of the three stages here, Playhouse, Opera House, and the Pit, caters to a different audience. Modern interpretations of Western classics by cutting-edge Japanese directors are highly regarded, though most foreign visitors prefer the more visual events like modern dance.
🔻 *Map A4 • 1-1-1 Honmachi, Shibuya-ku • 5351-3011 • Open 10am–7pm*

9 Bunkamura Theater Cocoon
Housed in the huge Bunkamura culture and arts center, the Cocoon hosts concerts, musicals, and opera. A medium-sized theater, it is best known for performances of contemporary dance, ballet, and a long involvement with flamenco dance and music troupes from Spain.
🔻 *Map Q5 • 2-24-1 Dogenzaka, Shibuya-ku • 3477-9111 • Open 10am–7pm*

Revivalist-style Kabuki-za Theater building

10 Kabuki-za Theater
Dating from 1949, this Baroque Japanese revivalist-style building stages Kabuki shows. Full dramas of three to four acts can extend throughout an afternoon or evening. Single-act tickets provide a shorter, more accessible entrée into Kabuki for the first timer (see p73).

Top 10 Films Set in Tokyo

1 Stray Dog (1949)
A rare chance to see what Tokyo's downtown streets looked like in the post-war era.

2 Tokyo Story (1953)
Yasujiro Ozu's classic, set mostly in a downtown area of the city, explores the collapse of the Japanese family.

3 Godzilla (1954)
Awakened by the A-bomb, the giant lizard stumbles through the city until pacified by Japanese scientists.

4 Diary of a Shinjuku Thief (1968)
Nagisa Oshima's film explores the minds of young Japanese radicals in this audacious film.

5 Akira (1988)
Set in the year 2030, Otomo Katsuhiro's full-length animation is based on his own four-volume comic book.

6 Tokyo Pop (1988)
Fran Rubel Kuzui's story of an American singer cast adrift in the world of Japanese pop.

7 Neon Genesis Evangelion (1997)
Anno Hideaki's apocalyptic fantasy, set in a city resembling Tokyo, is a cult classic.

8 Shall We Dance? (1997)
Tokyo night scenes form the backdrop to this story of a salaryman who finds a higher purpose in ballroom dancing.

9 Kill Bill 1 (2000)
A legendary samurai sword enables Uma Thurman to leave behind a trail of destruction in this Tarantino film.

10 Lost in Translation (2003)
A fine performance from Bill Murray, but Sofia Coppola's stereotypical view of Tokyo, is oddly dated.

上百千馬一独楽

 The annual Die Pratze Dance Festival is held at the Azabu Die Pratze theater in August.

Left **Drum Museum** Center **National Science Museum** Right **Ueno Zoo**

Children's Attractions

1 Drum Museum
This interactive museum has a collection of over 600 *taiko* (drums) from all over the world. The highlight are the Japanese festival drums. Skins with a blue sticker can be played, but with care, while those with a red mark cannot be touched. A stickerless drum can be played freely. • Map Q2 • 2-1-1 Nishi-Asakusa, Taito-ku • 3844-2141 • Open 9am–6pm Wed–Sun • Adm

2 Ghibli Museum
Hayao Miyazaki's animations, surreal landscapes, whimsical characters, and fanciful sets can be seen here. The galleries trace the development of an animation feature at the studio. • Map A2 • 1-1-83 Shimorenjaku, Mitaka-shi • 0570-055-777 • Open 10am–6pm Wed–Mon • Adm • www.ghibli-museum.jp

3 National Children's Castle
Divided into a hands-on section with a playhouse, fully equipped kitchen, and climbing frames, the castle sets aside a floor for music and instruments. The roof has unicycles, carts, and a jungle gym. • Map S5 • 5-53-1 Jingumae, Shibuya-ku • 3797-5666 • Open 10am–5:30pm Sat–Sun • Adm • www.kodommono-shiro.jp

4 Kidzania
Children under 12 can experience the working world of adults by role-playing in dozens of jobs, such as TV anchor, pizza chef, or cop in a realistic city setting. • Map D2 • Lalaport Toyosu, 2-4-9 Toyosu, Koto-ku • 05-7006-4646 • Open 10am–3pm, 4–9pm • Adm • www.kidzania.jp

5 Kite Museum
Over 2,000 kites, shaped variously as squids, Sumo wrestlers, and Mount Fuji, are displayed here. Some are illustrated with the faces of manga characters, samurai warriors, and Kabuki actors *(see p69)*.

6 National Science Museum
The model of a giant whale greets visitors to the museum, which has dinosaur displays, exhibits on botany, fossils, asteroids, and oceanography, among other attractions *(see p83)*.

7 Shinagawa Aquarium
Bemused hammerhead sharks and green turtles stare out from the tanks at visitors, and there is a dolphin show kids will adore. A long water tunnel leads under the paths of

Children playing inside the National Children's Castle

60 Children are encouraged to have a bash on drums from as far away as Sri Lanka and the Amazon basin at the Drum Museum.

Tokyo's Top 10

Water tunnel, Shinagawa Aquarium

stingrays, tropical fish, and giant manta rays. ✪ *Map C1 • 3-2-1 Katsushima, Shinagawa-ku • 3762-3433 • Open 10am–5pm Wed–Mon • Adm*

8 Tokyo Disney Resort

Mickey and pals will pull out all the stops for kids in this fantasyland of castles, magic mountains, haunted mansions, Polynesian villages, and 3-D cinemas. ✪ *Map B1 • 1-1 Maihama, Urayasu-shi • 04568-33333 • Open 8:30am–10pm • Adm*

9 Tokyo Dome City

This amusement park has a free-fall parachute ride, "Sky-flower," but the highlight is a rollercoaster, "Thunder Dolphin." LaQua, the park's other section, has eateries, shops, and spas. ✪ *Map E2 • 1-3-61 Koraku, Bunkyo-ku • 5800-9999 • Open 10am–10pm • Adm*

10 Ueno Zoo

Japan's oldest zoo, built in 1882, Ueno Zoo features pandas, gorillas, snow leopards, apes, and Bengal tigers. There is a monorail ride above the zoo to an animal petting zone. ✪ *Map F1 • 9-83 Ueno Koen, Taito-ku • 3828-5171 • Open 9:30am–5pm Tue–Sun • Adm*

Top 10 Kids' Shopping

1 Kiddyland

Six floors of toys, cuddly character models, and games. ✪ *Map S4 • 6-1-9 Jingumae, Shibuya-ku • 3409-3431*

2 Crayon House

A family center with a restaurant, toys, and books. ✪ *Map C5 • 3-8-15 Kita-Aoyama, Minato-ku • 3406-6409*

3 Hakuhinkan Toy Park

The latest models, characters, games, and restaurants. ✪ *Map M5 • 8-8-11 Ginza, Chuo-ku • 3571-8008*

4 BorneLund

No synthetic items, only wooden imports. ✪ *Map S4 • Hara Bldg, 1F, 6-10-9 Jingumae, Shibuya-ku • 5485-3430*

5 Yamashiroya Toy Shop

Old-fashioned, no-frills shop, but well stocked. ✪ *Map F2 • Ueno, Taito-ku • 3831-2320*

6 Tsukumo Robocon Magazine Kan

Specialist in small robots of animals. ✪ *Map F3 • Yamaguchi Bldg, 1F, 3-2-13, Soto-Kanda, Chiyoda-ku • 3251-0987*

7 Aso Bit City

Fun electronic goods, train sets, and manga characters. ✪ *Map F3 • 4-3-3 Soto-Kanda, Chiyoda-ku • 3251-3100*

8 Sayegusa

Children's clothes and accessories. ✪ *Map M5 • 7-8-8 Ginza, Chuo-ku*

9 Pokémon Center

The best merchandise of the "Pocket Monsters" anime series *(see p44).*

10 Kuramae–Asakusabashi Toy Street

Wholesalers showcase their wares along this traditional toy street. Some shops sell direct. ✪ *Map G3 • Kuramae, Taito-ku*

Tokyo's Top 10

*Sign up for DK's email newsletter on **traveldk.com***

61

Left **Oto** Right **Blue Note Tokyo**

Music Clubs

1 Blue Note Tokyo

Cognoscenti claim this Tokyo branch – Japan's most famous jazz club – is just as good as sister venues in Paris or New York. Some of the world's hottest acts play here; the medium to short sets cover jazz, fusion, world music, and soul. ✪ Map C6
• 6-3-16 Minami-Aoyama, Minato-ku
• 5485-0088 • Call for timings of shows
• Adm • www.bluenote.co.jp

2 Bar Matrix

Named after the Hollywood movie *Matrix*, Bar Matrix caters to an international crowd. It plays warm, feel-good sounds of reggae, hip hop, rock, R&B, and trance. Don't pass up the club's great bar. For a taste of what is on offer, sample drinks during happy hour (6–10pm). ✪ Map D6
• Mizobuchi Bldg, B1F, 3-13-6 Roppongi, Minato-ku • 3405-1066 • Open 6pm–4am

3 328 (San Ni Pa)

A long-established fixture on the Tokyo club scene, 328 draws on a legacy that goes back to the

People enjoying drinks at 328 (San Ni Pa)

late 1970s. This small, often packed venue brings together a spectrum of sounds from soul and R&B to post-punk, electro, and dance classics from the golden age of disco. ✪ Map D6
• B1F, 3-24-20 Nishi-Azabu, Minato-ku
• 3401-4968 • Open 8pm–5am • Adm

4 Shinjuku Pit Inn

One of the oldest jazz clubs in Tokyo, this place was recently renewed. However, this medium-sized venue hasn't altered its musical tastes, which tend toward fusion and new direction jazz. Traditional bands also get an airing. International and local acts perform here. One drink is included in the entry fee. ✪ Map B3 • 2-12-4 Accor Bldg, B1 Shinjuku
• 3354-2024 • Open 6:30–10pm • Adm

5 Shinjuku Loft

A well-established club, Shinjuku Loft offers a varied menu of acts, events, and performers. The bands play loudly, but there are softer DJ nights, with local and, occasionally, international spinners. The club is divided into a main stage where groups play, and a small platform area for hanging out near the bar (see p106).

6 Womb

Devotees of techno, house, and drum 'n' bass will love this club, which has one of the largest

Dancers on the floor at Womb

dance floors in the city. A huge mirror ball hangs over the dance area, adding to an already impressive lighting system. Air-jet blasters keep things cool. The club sprawls over four floors, each with its own bar. ✉ *Map Q6 • 2-16 Maruyamacho, Shibuya-ku • 5459-0039 • Open 9pm–5am • Adm • www. womb.co.jp*

Club Harlem

The biggest hip hop club in Tokyo, Harlem runs its own magazine and record label. Rap, R&B, and funk also get played by local DJ heroes, such as Ken Bo and DJ Toyo. Harlem is the place to visit for those eager to know about Japan's hip hop scene. ✉ *Map Q6 • Dr. Jekaahn's Bldg, 2F-3F, 23-4 Maruyamacho, Shibuya-ku • 3461-8806 • Open 10pm–5am Tue–Sat • Adm • www. harlem.co.jp*

Salsa Sudada

Salsa has been a fixture on the Tokyo club scene for a lot longer than most people think. Salsa Sudada is one of several Latin clubs in the city, attracting a crowd of local patrons, as well as Brazilian, Colombian, and Peruvian expatriates. Dance lessons are held every night for the uninitiated at this friendly place *(see p92)*.

Shibuya Nuts

The controlling sounds at Shibuya Nuts – much like its sister club Roppongi Nuts – are reggae and hip hop, with a smattering of house. "Raga Nuts" is a Sunday night special featuring mostly reggae tracks. Visiting MCs from Jamaica often host the shows, adding color and authenticity to the sounds. ✉ *Map R6 • B2, 2-17-3 Shibuya, Shibuya-ku • 5466-8814 • Open 10am–5pm Tue–Sun • Adm*

Oto

A long, narrow room that would seem to restrict dance, Oto turns out to be a surprisingly good place to hit the floor. A dazzling PA system runs a mix of strong R&B, reggae, and hip hop dance rhythms, served up by local and international DJs *(see p106)*.

AROUND TOWN

TOKYO'S TOP 10

Left **Exhibition Hall, Bridgestone Museum of Art** Right **Tokyo Station**

Central Tokyo

HE HISTORIC CITY and the site of Edo Castle, with its moats, stone
ramparts, and bridges, once defined the imperial power structure with the
merchant classes to the east, and samurai and lords to the south and west. In
some ways, the power structure has remained visibly intact, with the Imperial
Palace at the center; parliament, law courts, and police headquarters to the
south; and the financial center to the east. The area has been transformed by
a series of fires, earthquakes, air raids, and devel-
opers, yet the outlines of the core city remain intact.
This district has become a lively tourist attraction.

🔟 Sights

1 Imperial Palace East Gardens
2 Crafts Gallery
3 Bridgestone Museum of Art
4 Tokyo Station
5 Marunouchi Building
6 Nihonbashi Bridge
7 Bank of Japan
8 Tokyo Stock Exchange
9 Kite Museum
10 Tokyo Station Gallery

Nihonbashi Bridge

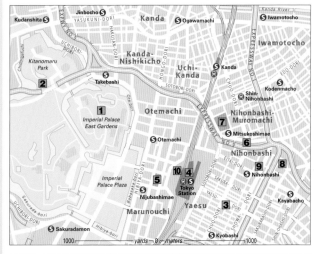

Preceding pages **Tsurugaoka Hachimangu Temple in Kamakura**

East Gardens, with view to the tea pavilion

1 Imperial Palace East Gardens

Designed by Kobori Enshu in the 17th century, the gardens were restored in 1968. The nucleus of this design can be seen in the pond area, with its waterfall, stone lantern, bridge, tea pavilion, and pebbled beach. The garden is resplendent with plum blossoms, spring cherry, and azaleas in late winter; irises and lilies in summer; and bush clover, camellias, and maple leaves in the fall. ❧ *Map L2 • Chiyoda, Chiyoda-ku • Open 9am–4:30pm Tue–Thu, Sat–Sun*

2 Crafts Gallery

Beautifully finished in brick and stonework, the 1910 building housing this museum once served as the headquarters of the Imperial Guard. Today, it showcases *mingei*, folk craft products representing a mid-20th-century movement that saw beauty through the use and aging of objects. There are fine examples of pottery, textiles, ceramics, lacquer, glass, metal and bamboo ware. Exhibitions tend to focus on single themes, individual artists working with traditional methods, and materials. ❧ *Map K1 • 1-1 Kitanomaru-koen, Chiyoda-ku • 5777-8600 • Open 10am–5pm Tue–Sun • Adm*

3 Bridgestone Museum of Art

This important museum was built in 1952, when the city was still emerging from the rubble of defeat. The Japanese love of all things Gallic is reflected in the collection of mostly French Impressionist paintings, including some rare works by Matisse and Renoir. Also featured are ancient Greek sculpture, European Modernism and Abstraction, and some Japanese Impressionist works. ❧ *Map N3 • 1-10-1 Kyobashi, Chuo-ku • 3563-0241 • Open 10am–8pm Tue–Sat, 10am–6pm Sun • Adm*

4 Tokyo Station

Designed by Tatsuno Kingo, this 1914 building marks an advance in modern Japanese architecture in the Western manner. Rendered in the Queen Anne style, it is said to be modeled after Amsterdam Centraal Station. Thanks to its steel frame, the building survived the great 1923 earthquake, but lost its two upper stories and cupolas in WWII. These are now being restored. ❧ *Map N3 • 1-9-1 Marunouchi, Chiyoda-ku*

Elegant exterior of the Crafts Gallery

Remnants of the original Edo Castle fortifications survive in the Imperial Palace East Gardens.

The soaring Marunouchi Building

Marunouchi Building

Known as the "Marubiru," this structure was the first in the area permitted to overlook the Imperial Palace grounds. The restaurants at the top of this 36-story building offer spectacular views. The current building retains a footprint of the original pre-war structure in its five-story podium and the triple arches built into the façade. The basement and first four floors are lined with gourmet food stores, restaurants, boutiques, and the American pharmacy. ® *Map M3 • 2-4-1 Marunouchi, Chiyoda-ku • 5218-5100*

Nihonbashi Bridge

Occupying a special place in Tokyo's history, the Nihonbashi is shown in many old *ukiyo-e* woodblock prints. The current structure dates from 1911. In the run-up to the Tokyo Olympics in 1964, canals and rivers were filled in and a system of overhead expressways built. Distances throughout Japan are still measured from the bronze pole here, called the Zero Kilometer marker. ® *Map P2 • Nihonbashi, Chuo-ku*

Building Edo Castle

In 1640, when Edo Castle was completed, it was the largest citadel in the world, with 30 bridges, 28 armories, 21 watchtowers, and 110 gates. Gigantic slabs of stone were shipped from the Izu peninsula to make impregnable walls. More than 100 men were hired to drag the stones from the ship. The stones have survived; the wooden castle has not.

Bank of Japan

The bank was aptly built on the site of the shogun's former gold, silver, and copper mints. Tatsuno Kingo, who designed Tokyo Station, was responsible for this earlier 1896 building. The bank is divided into two sections of equal age but called the New Building and the Old Building. The former is where financial transactions occur, the latter, with a few offices, is more of an architectural exhibit. The building represents the first Western-style building by a Japanese architect. ® *Map N2 • 2-1-1 Nihonbashi-Hongokucho, Chuo-ku • 3279-1111 • Tours: 9:45am–3pm*

Tokyo Stock Exchange

Business is now done by computers without a trading floor, a far cry from the early days when trading hours were measured by burning a length of rope. You can read stock prices and names as they appear on a giant glass cylinder. A 40-minute guided tour in English touches on the history and purpose of the exchange. ® *Map P3 • 2-1 Nihonbashi Kabutocho, Chuo-ku • 3665-1881 • Open 9am–4pm Mon–Fri; tours: 1:30pm*

Tokyo Stock Exchange

The Bank of Japan offers free tours in English. It is advisable to reserve a tour at least a week in advance.

Kite Museum

9 Displaying over 20,000 kites from all over the world, the museum focuses on Japan and China. The Japanese kites are adorned with real and mythological figures, as well as animals and natural landscapes such as waves and sacred mountains. Kite frames are made from bamboo, and the sails from *washi*, a strong paper made from a type of mulberry tree. Picture outlines are painted in black *sumi* ink to restrict the flow of color pigments. ⊗ *Map P3 • Taimeiken 5F, 1-12-10 Nihonbashi, Chuo-ku • 3271-2465 • Open 11am–5pm Mon–Sat • Adm • www.tako.gr.jp*

A colorful display at the Kite Museum

Tokyo Station Gallery

10 This small but interesting gallery is part of the original 1914 station. The walls, like the building, are made of brick, a unique but apt surface for the paintings and photos that are hung here. Set up in 1988 to expand the function of the station into a cultural venue, the gallery features a lot of Japanese oils and watercolors, as well as some international art. ⊗ *Map N3 • 1-9-1 Marunouchi, Chiyoda-ku • 3212-2485 • Open 10am–7pm Tue–Fri, 10am–6pm Sat–Sun • Adm*

A Day Exploring Historical Sites

Morning

Arrive at **Kudanshita Station** around 10am after the commuter crowds have dispersed. Exit the station on Yasukuni-dori avenue, take a sharp left, where the 1930s **Kudan Kaikan Hotel** *(see p49)* stands, a blend of nativist and Art Deco styles. Return to the main road and walk uphill to the **Yasukuni Shrine** *(see p37)*, a fine piece of Shinto architecture. Forego the military museum in favor of strolling the pleasant grounds, full of cherry trees. Have tea beside the garden pond, or wind back to the Kudan Kaikan for one of their afternoon tea sets. The rooftop beer garden with a view is another option.

Afternoon

Return to the main road, cross, and follow the signpost to Tayasu-mon, a wooden gate leading into Kitanomaru Park. Before seeing the gate, note an old Meiji-era tower. Past the gate, linger outside the octagonal **Budokan** *(see p8)*, the martial arts hall where the Beatles once gave a concert. Follow the road south to the pretty **Imperial Palace East Gardens** *(see p67)*, the former site of **Edo Castle**, the shogun's citadel. Here you can climb the ruins of a keep for a view of the gardens. Press on south toward the **Babasaki Moat**, home to white swans, egrets, and turtles. Cross busy Hibiya-dori and walk toward the nearby **Tokyo Station** *(see p67)*, a superb 1914 structure. Have a drink at the Mandarin Bar in the Mandarin Oriental Hotel *(see p126)*.

Left **Pokémon Center** Center **Takashimaya** Right **Mitsukoshi department store**

TOP 10 Shopping

1 Shin Marunouchi Building
The expansive shopping mall in this skyscraper has more than 150 stores, including boutiques and bakeries. ✆ Map M3 • 1-5-1 Marunouchi, Chiyoda-ku • 5218-5100

2 Takashimaya
This upmarket store stocks classic men's and women's clothing, as well as furniture and exquisite Japanese crafts. ✆ Map P3 • 2-4-1 Nihonbashi, Chuo-ku • 3211-4111

3 Mitsukoshi
The flagship branch of Japan's oldest department store sells clothes, jewelry, household goods, textiles, and crafts. ✆ Map P2 • 1-4-1 Marumachi, Nihonbashi, Chuo-ku • 3241-3311

4 Oazo
This dazzling glass complex of stores, restaurants, and cafés also has a massive English bookstore, Maruzen. ✆ Map N2 • 1-6-4 Marunouchi, Chiyoda-ku • 5218-5100

5 Mujirushi Ryohin
This "no-brand goods" store has become a byword for stylish, good-value clothes, furnishings, and housewares. ✆ Map N3 • 3-8-3 Marunouchi, Chiyoda-ku • 5208-8241

6 Pokémon Center
The main showcase for "Pocket Monsters" merchandizing, the center also stocks new computer games for kids. ✆ Map P3 • 2F, Shiba-Rikyu Bldg, 1-2-3 Shiodome, Minato-ku • 6430-7733

7 Ebisu-Do Gallery
This gallery specializes in ukiyo-e woodblock prints. Originals start at ¥25,000, good reproductions at only ¥3,000. ✆ Map E3 • Kamesawa Bldg, 2F, 1-12 Kanda-Jimbocho, Chiyoda-ku • 3219-7651

8 Yamamoto Yama
In addition to fine-quality Japanese and Chinese teas, tea ceremony instruments such as bamboo whisks, iron water pots, and ceramic tea bowls can be bought here. ✆ Map P3 • 2-5-2 Nihonbashi, Chuo-ku • 3281-0010

9 Ohya Shobo
Established in 1882, this store sells ukiyo-e woodblock prints and antiquarian books at reasonable prices. ✆ Map E3 • 1-1 Kanda-Jimbocho, Chiyoda-ku • 3291-0062

10 Isseido
Dating from 1913, this antiquarian bookstore retains all its original Art Deco features. The second floor has old English books and rare maps. ✆ Map E3 • 1-7 Kanda-Jimbocho, Chiyoda-ku • 3292-0071.

The Mitsukoshi department store has an exceptional section on kimono.

Price Categories

Price ranges are for an average-size dinner for one. Lunchtime menus are often less expensive.

¥	Under ¥2,000
¥¥	¥2,000–¥5,000
¥¥¥	¥5,000–¥10,000
¥¥¥¥	Over ¥10,000

Left **Dhaba India** Right **Aroyna Tabeta**

🔟 Places to Eat

1 Brasserie aux Amis
Rustic brasserie food in a charming setting. Wash down your *plat de jour poisson* with a drink from the long wine list. ◈ *Map M3 • Shin-Tokyo Bldg, 1F, 3-3-1 Marunouchi, Chiyoda-ku • 6212-1566 • ¥¥*

2 Bar de España Muy
Fun tapas bar seving Catalan-style food. Try the black squid with a glass of cava. ◈ *Map M3 • Tokyo Bldg Tokia, 2F, 2-7-3 Marunouchi, Chiyoda-ku • 5224-6161 • ¥¥*

3 Dhaba India
This southern Indian eatery offers thali sets and masala dosas served with basmati rice. ◈ *Map N3 • 2-7-9 Yaesu, Chuo-ku • 3272-7160 • ¥*

4 Breeze of Tokyo
French and Japanese cuisine meet in a chic setting. An extensive list of cocktails and wines and 30 different types of champagne. ◈ *Map M3 • Marunouchi Bldg, 36F, 2-4-1 Marunouchi, Chiyoda-ku • 5220-5551 • ¥¥*

5 Kua' Aina
Hawaiian-style hamburgers, avocado salads, and microbrews are served in this modern Polynesian joint. ◈ *Map M3 • 5F, Marunouchi Bldg, 2-4-1 Marunouchi, Chiyoda-ku • 5220-2440 • ¥*

6 Aroyna Tabeta
This modest eatery serves tasty spicy green and red curries and fried noodles. ◈ *Map M3 • 3-7-11 Marunouchi, Chiyoda-ku • 5219-6099 • ¥*

7 Yukari
Known for its delicately prepared fish dishes with mouthwatering relishes and seasoning. Try the conger eel, snapper, and crab with Japanese citrus for starters. ◈ *Map N3 • 3-2-14 Nihonbashi, Chuo-ku • 3271-3436 • Closed Sun • ¥¥*

8 Mikuni's Café Marunouchi
Healthy Italian grub in a modern setting. Don't miss the bakery annex for fresh breads and desserts. ◈ *Map M3 • 2-6-1 Marunouchi, Chiyoda-ku • 5220-3921 • ¥*

9 Salt
Crisp Australian wines are perfect compliments for the fusion food with the stress on fish. ◈ *Map M3 • Shin-Marunouchi Bldg, 5F, 1-5-1 Marunouchi, Chiyoda-ku • 5288-7828 • Closed Sun • ¥¥*

10 En
A fine selection of regional Japanese cuisine and simple dishes such as grilled salmon belly and smoky eggplant. ◈ *Map N2 • Oazo Bldg, 5F, 1-6-4, Marunouchi, Oazo, Chiyoda-ku • 5223-9896 • ¥¥*

Left **Sony Building** Right **ADMT Advertising Museum**

The Ginza

THE SITE OF THE SHOGUN'S *original silver mint, the Ginza has always been synonymous with commerce and wealth. After a disastrous fire in 1872, the government commissioned the English architect Thomas Waters to rebuild the district in brick. The new quarter established the Ginza as a leader in commerce, leisure, and fashion. It was the site of Japan's first gas lamps, trolley cars, and Western-style department stores. The epicenter of the Ginza is the 4-chome*

Striking façade of the Kabuki-za Theater

district, a crossing dominated by modern stores. A premier cosmopolitan shopping and culture experience, with its teahouses, incense and calligraphy shops, high-end sushi restaurants, and the very traditional Kabuki-za Theater, it is also firmly Japanese.

🔟 Sights

1. Sony Building
2. Kabuki-za Theater
3. National Film Center
4. Idemitsu Museum of Arts
5. Hibiya Park
6. Tokyo International Forum
7. Shiodome and Caretta Shiodome
8. ADMT Advertising Museum
9. Hama Rikyu Garden
10. Tsukiji Fish Market

1 Sony Building

Catch a glimpse of the shape and sound of things to come at this eight-story showcase for Sony models and new technologies. You can test the hottest games at the free PlayStation arcade on the sixth floor with its video and virtual reality sites. The two-floor basement area, the Sony Plaza, has novelties and fun items for sale. Parents can withdraw to one of the Hi-Vision Theaters. ◈ *Map M4 • 5-3-1 Ginza, Chuo-ku • 3573-2563 • Open 11am–7pm*

2 Kabuki-za Theater

The current incarnation of the theater dates from 1950, when it was rebuilt after being damaged in an air raid. The model was the short-lived 1925 version, based on a Momoyama-era design from the medieval period. The resulting fusion of classical Japanese and Western architecture is distinctive. Banners hung above the entrance, red lanterns, and garish posters add to the building's theatricality. Some of the older architectural features will be kept in the new Kabuki-za, due for completion in 2013, including the *hanamachi* (flower path), a runway extending into the audience. During the construction at the same site, performances will take place at the Shimbashi Embujo *(see pp58–9)*. ◈ *Map N5 • 4-12-15 Ginza, Chuo-ku • 3541-3131*

3 National Film Center

Connected to the National Museum of Modern Art, the NFC is Japan's only center devoted to the study and dissemination of Japanese and foreign films. The NFC holds almost 40,000 films in its collection, including many restored Japanese classics.

Glass-fronted exterior, National Film Center

Besides its two theaters, there is a fourth-floor library of books on film, a seventh-floor gallery featuring exhibitions of photos, stills, and film-related items, and a café. They sometimes run programs of Japanese masterpieces with English subtitles. ◈ *Map N4 • 3-7-6 Kyobashi, Chuo-ku • 3561-0823 • Call for timings • Adm • www.momat.go.jp*

4 Idemitsu Museum of Arts

As petroleum tycoon Idemitsu Sazo's fortune increased, so did his passion for collecting Japanese and Asian art. Opened in 1966, the museum has a diverse, eclectic collection, which includes paintings, bronzes, ceramic ware, *ukiyo-e* paintings, lacquer, and rare gold-painted screens. Its calligraphy holdings include the world's largest collection of works by the Zen monk Sengai. Works from China, Korea, and the Middle East are also periodically displayed. A room full of pottery shards affords tremendous ninth-floor views of the Imperial Palace grounds. ◈ *Map M4 • Teigeki Bldg, 9F, 3-1-1 Marunouchi, Chiyoda-ku • 3213-9402 • Open 10am–5pm Tue–Sun (10am–7pm Fri) • Adm • www.idemitsu.co.jp/museum*

5 Hibiya Park

Built over a former military parade ground converted from the estates of shogun Ieyasu's less-favored Outer Lords, Hibiya Park was rebuilt as Japan's first Western-style park in 1903. European features, such as bandstands, a rose garden, an open-air theater, and a bronze heron fountain overlooked by a wisteria trellis, are set against a small but exquisite Japanese garden, rock placements, and cherry trees lining parts of secluded paths at the center of the park. ◉ Map L4 • Hibiya koen, 1-6 Chiyoda-ku • 3501-6428

6 Tokyo International Forum

One of the city's architectural wonders, this majestic building was designed by Rafael Vinoly in 1996. It functions as a premier culture convention center, with four graduated cubes encased in granite, abutting a high, tapering trajectory of glass and steel, aptly named the "Glass Hall." Crossing the skywalks among the glass and girders at the transparent apex of the building, above cantilevered areas and atrias, is like walking across a crystal space above the city. ◉ Map M3 • 3-5-1 Marunouchi, Chiyoda-ku • 5221-9000 • www.t-i-forum. co.jp/english

Caretta Shiodome

7 Shiodome and Caretta Shiodome

A futuristic mini-city, the bayside Shiodome features a grove of skyscrapers, notably Shiodome Media Tower and the highly regarded Conrad Tokyo hotel, as well as an Italian-style outdoor piazza, cafés, restaurants, and cocktail bars. The 51-story Caretta Shiodome houses more than 60 shops, restaurants, and cafés linked by underground concourses to other shopping venues. ◉ Map M5 • 1-8-2 Higashi-Shimbashi, Minato-ku • 6218-2100

8 ADMT Advertising Museum

Sponsored by advertising giant Dentsu, this outstanding museum traces the history of Japanese advertising. Exhibits run from colored woodblock prints to the latest TV commercials. The museum library, Japan's only archive exclusively dedicated to

Taisho Chic

Popular culture thrived along the Ginza during the Taisho period (1912–26), as a more liberal mood blew through the city. The age saw the appearance of the "Modern Girl," a product of European fashions, the American Jazz Age, and the film divas. In their Eton crops and bobbed hair, these girls typified the confidence and style of a new age that challenged traditional Japanese values.

The ultra-modern Tokyo International Forum

A colorful chrysanthemum festival is held at the rear of the Hibiya Park during late October through November.

advertising, has over 150,000 digitally saved advertisements. ✆ *Map M5 • Caretta Shiodome, 1-8-2 Higashi-Shimbashi, B1F-B2F, Minato-ku • 6218-2500 • Open 11am–6:30pm Tue–Fri, 11am–4:30pm Sat • www.admt.jp*

Hama Rikyu's detached garden

🔟 Hama Rikyu Garden
The younger brother of shogun Ietsuna had parts of the bay filled in and a villa built here in 1654. Completed by a later shogun, Ienari, the basic design and balance of the garden remain gloriously intact. The highlight is a large tidal pond, with a small tea pavilion, and islets connected by wooden bridges. Over 600 species of peony, in addition to crape myrtle, cherry, irises, bamboo, and plum, grow in the garden today. ✆ *Map M6 • 1-1 Hama-Rikyu Teien, Chuo-ku • 3541-0200 • Open 9am–5pm • Adm*

🔟 Tsukiji Fish Market
More than 400 different kinds of seafood arrive every day for auctioning and dispatching at Tsukiji, also called the Tokyo Central Wholesale Market. Eels come from Taiwan, salmon from Chile and Canada, tuna from Tasmania, and shrimp from Thailand. A grid of small shops sells knives, kitchen utensils, cheap crockery, and bamboo goods. Some sections are off-limits to visitors. ✆ *Map N6 • Tsukiji, Chuo-ku • Closed 2nd & 4th Wed*

A Day Shopping in the Ginza

Morning

🕐 Leaving the Ginza station at the 4-chome exit well before 10am, have coffee at the elegant **Le Café Doutor Ginza**. Walk across to the **Mitsukoshi** department store opposite, where the grand clock sounds 10am. Stroll a few steps to the svelte **Christian Dior Building**, and then return to the 4-chome crossing. **Wako**, a symbol of the Ginza since the early 1930s, stands on the opposite corner. Next door, the bakery **Kimuraya** specializes in *anpan*, a local delicacy since 1875. Return to Mitsukoshi, with its trademark bronze lion, known for high-quality goods. Spare a few minutes to ascend to the roof, where offerings are left at a Shinto shrine to promote prosperity. Descend to the cornucopic food basement for a light lunch or green tea and Japanese sweets.

Afternoon

Cross the road and walk northeast along **Chuo-dori**, the main shopping vector, passing **Mikimoto**, the originator of cultured pearls, until you reach **Maronnier-dori**. Turn left and you will see **Printemps**, a branch of the Paris-based *grand magasin*. Return to Chuo-dori, cross the road and turn right where **Matsuya** sells Japanese souvenirs. Return to 4-chome, cross the road, and stop by at the **Nissan Gallery** with the newest car models on display. Proceed to **Matsuzakaya**, another chic department store. Repair at the famous **Lion Beer Hall** nearby (*see p55*).

Left **Shiseido Gallery** Center **Nikon Plaza Ginza** Right **INAX Gallery**

Galleries

1 Tokyo Gallery
Expect new works from Japanese, Korean, and Chinese artists. English-speaking staff. ✪ *Map M5 • Daiwa Shunya Bldg, 7F, 8-10-5 Ginza, Chuo-ku • 3571-1808 • Open 11am–7pm Mon–Fri, 11am–5pm Sat*

2 Galleria Grafica Tokyo
New works are shown by young artists on the first floor, while prints and lithographs from greats such as Picasso grace the second floor. ✪ *Map M5 • Ginza S2 Bldg 1, 2F, 6-13-4 Ginza, Chuo-ku • 5550-1335 • Open 11am–7pm Mon–Sat*

3 Vanilla Gallery
Erotic art gallery featuring Japanese and overseas exhibits. ✪ *Map M5 • 4F, 6-10-10 Ginza, Chuo-ku • 5568-1233 • Open noon–7pm Mon–Fri, noon–5pm Sat*

4 Shiseido Gallery
Contemporary Japanese and international artists, retrospectives, and fashion-linked exhibitions are featured. ✪ *Map M5 • B1, 8-8-3 Ginza, Chuo-ku • 3572-3901 • Open 11am–7pm Tue–Sat, 11am–6pm Sun*

5 Gallery Koyanagi
Leading Japanese and international photo and print artists are showcased. ✪ *Map N4 • 1-7-5 Ginza, Chuo-ku • 3561-1896 • Open 11am–7pm Tue–Sat*

6 Wacoal Ginza Art Space
Specializing in fabrics and ceramic materials, Wacoal underwrites this gallery and its exhibits. ✪ *Map M4 • Miyuki No.1 Bldg, B1, 5-1-15 Ginza, Chuo-ku • 3573-3798 • Open 11am–7pm Mon–Fri, 11am–5pm Sat*

7 Ginza Graphic Gallery
Sponsored by one of Japan's largest printing outfits, the gallery features Japanese graphic designers. ✪ *Map M5 • DNP Ginza Bldg, 1F, 7-7-2 Ginza, Chuo-ku • 3571-5206 • Open 11am–7pm Mon–Fri, 11am–6pm Sat*

8 Nikon Plaza Ginza
Contemporary and retrospective shows by Japanese and international artists. ✪ *Map M5 • 1F, Strata Ginza, 10-1-7, Ginza, Chuo-ku • 5537-1469 • Open 11am–7pm Tue–Sun*

9 INAX Gallery
Works by new, craft-oriented artists and world craft techniques. ✪ *Map N4 • INAX Ginza Showroom, 9F, 3-6-18 Kyobashi, Chuo-ku • 5250-6530 • Open 10am–6pm Mon–Sat*

10 Sakai Kokodo Gallery
This gallery has exhibited *ukiyo-e* woodblock prints since 1870. ✪ *Map M4 • Murasaki Bldg, 1F, 1-2-14 Yurakucho, Chiyoda-ku • 3591-4678 • Open 11am–6pm*

Nikon models and products can be viewed in the showroom at Nikon Plaza Ginza.

Left **Items for sale, Kyukyodo** Right **Akebono**

🔟 Specialist Stores

1 Hakuhinkan
Tokyo's largest toy store is stuffed with cutesy Japanese character toys, cuddly animals, the latest video games, and child-friendly restaurants. ✎ *Map M5 • 8-8-11 Ginza, Chuo-ku • 3571-8008*

2 Akebono
The store specializes in *akebono*, traditional Japanese sweets made from sweet potato and beans, best eaten with green tea. ✎ *Map M4 • 5-7-19 Ginza, Chuo-ku • 3571-3640*

3 Mikimoto Ginza 2
An eye-catching building designed by Ito Toyo, Mikimoto 2 sells the type of exquisite cultured pearls first invented by Mikimoto Koichi in 1893. ✎ *Map N4 • 2-4-12 Ginza, Chuo-ku • 3562-3130*

4 Sayegusa
Top-quality children's wear store that has been in business since 1869. Four floors of clothing, dresses, suits, and accessories. ✎ *Map M5 • 7-8-8 Ginza, Chuo-ku • 3573-2441*

5 Kimuraya
Set up in the 1870s, Kimuraya sells *anpan*, bread rolls stuffed with red bean paste. ✎ *Map M4 • 4-5-7 Ginza, Chuo-ku • 3561-0091*

6 Takumi
An interesting mix of folk crafts, ceramics, and traditional toys in a tasteful setting. ✎ *Map M5 • 8-2-4 Ginza, Chuo-ku • 3571-2017*

7 Ginza Natsuno
A small store with a huge selection of all manner of chopsticks. Light and portable, they make ideal souvenirs. ✎ *Map M5 • 6-7-4 Ginza, Chuo-ku • 3569-0952*

8 Kyukyodo
A venerable Japanese paper specialist, Kyukyodo has been in the trade since the 17th century. Gift cards, paper boxes, and incense are also on sale. ✎ *Map M4 • 5-7-4 Ginza, Chuo-ku • 3571-4429*

9 Niwaka
Besides original, custom-designed jewelry created by artisans in Kyoto workshops, Niwaka also has a made-to-order service for those who wish to design their own jewelry. ✎ *Map N4 • 2-8-18 Ginza, Chuo-ku • 3564-0707*

10 Tanagokoro
Purveyors of *binchotan*, a high-quality charcoal. Placed in a room or bath water, it is said to have curative powers and can also act as a purifier, humidifier, and deodorizer. ✎ *Map N4 • 1-8-15 Ginza, Chuo-ku • 3538-6555*

At Takumi, explanations in English about the background and creation of items are supplied with purchases.

Left **Ten-Ichi Deux** Center **Daiwa Sushi** Right **Sushiko Honten**

Fish Restaurants

1 Kyubei
The high temple of sushi, Kyubei offers a memorable eating experience, even when it breaks the bank. ⊗ *Map M5 • 8-7-6 Ginza, Chuo-ku • 3571-6523 • Closed Sun • ¥¥¥¥*

2 Ten-Ichi
Tokyo's most rated, celebrity-endorsed tempura restaurant serves light, delicately fried fish and vegetable morsels direct from the pan. ⊗ *Map M5 • 6-6-5 Ginza, Chuo-ku • 3571-1949 • ¥¥¥¥*

3 Ten-Ichi Deux
The deep-fried tempura seafood and vegetables are served in a relaxed, café-style interior. ⊗ *Map M4 • Nishi Ginza Depato, 1F, 4-1 Ginza, Chuo-ku • 3566-4188 • ¥¥*

4 Daiwa Sushi
Lines are the norm at this early-hour Tsukiji raw fish venue. It's worth the wait for what many regard as the market's finest sushi bar. ⊗ *Map N6 • Bldg. 6, 5-2-1 Tsukiji, Ginza, Chuo-ku • 3547-6807 • Closed Sun • ¥¥*

5 Ginza Hokake
Delectable sushi, seaweed rolls, and sashimi are served to high standards in an old-fashioned, relaxed interior. ⊗ *Map N4 • 4-7-13 Ginza, Chuo-ku • 3564-2491 • ¥¥¥¥*

6 Kondo
Counter seating only for chef Fumio Kondo's exquisite tempura preparations. Besides fish, he has a creative line in batter-fried lotus root, asparagus, and other vegetables. ⊗ *Map M5 • Sakaguchi Bldg, 9F, 5-5-13 Ginza, Chuo-ku • 5568-0923 • Closed Sun • ¥¥¥¥*

7 Sushi Bun
Some of the freshest fish in town served at a counter in the heart of the market. Excellent sushi set meal. ⊗ *Map N6 • Chuo Shijo Bldg. No.8, 5-2-1 Tsukiji, Chuo-ku • 3541-3860 • Closed Sun • ¥¥*

8 Edogin
Fresh from tanks in the dining area, the sushi could not be fresher. Plentiful servings in a spacious, no-frills, and boisterous setting. ⊗ *Map N5 • 4-5-1 Tsukiji, Chuo-ku • 3543-4401 • ¥¥¥*

9 Tsukiji Sushi-sei
Ask for the reliable *omakase* (chef's choice) at this traditional, Edo-style sushi chain. ⊗ *Map N5 • 4-13-9 Tsukiji, Chuo-ku • 3541-7720 • Closed Sun • ¥¥¥*

10 Sushiko Honten
High-end sushi spot with just 11 counter seats. There is no menu, so it is best to just follow the chef's recommendations for the day. ⊗ *Map M4 • 6-3-8 Ginza, Chuo-ku • 3571-1968 • ¥¥¥¥*

Recommend your favorite restaurant on **traveldk.com**

Price Categories

Price ranges are for an average-size dinner for one. Lunchtime menus are often less expensive.	¥ Under ¥2,000
	¥¥ ¥2,000–¥5,000
	¥¥¥ ¥5,000–¥10,000
	¥¥¥¥ Over ¥10,000

Left **Skewered *yakitori* platter at Bird Land** Right **Little Okinawa**

🔟 Places to Eat

1 Dazzle
The sparkling interior, glass-fronted wine cellar, bar, and sumptuous decor almost upstage the delicious fusion dishes. ◎ *Map N4 • Mikimoto Ginza 2, 8-9 F, 2-4-12 Ginza, Chuo-ku • 5159-0991 • ¥¥¥*

2 Robata
Japanese country food, including grilled food, tofu dishes, and salads, served in a rustic setting. ◎ *Map M4 • 1-3-8 Yurakucho, Chiyoda-ku • 3591-1905 • ¥¥*

3 Azumitei
Grill or dip the meat into a simmering cauldron at your own table at this modern *sukiyaki* and *shabu-shabu* eatery. ◎ *Map M4 • Ginza Inz 1 Bldg, 2F, 3-1 Saki Ginza-Nishi, Chuo-ku • 5524-7890 • ¥¥¥*

4 Little Okinawa
Southern island cuisine includes Okinawa-style pork and noodle dishes. Perfect with *awamori*, a fiery, rice-based Okinawan spirit. ◎ *Map M5 • 8-7-10 Ginza, Chuo-ku • 3572-2930 • ¥¥*

5 Under the Tracks Yakitori
Try grilled and charbroiled chicken with spicy sauces and herbs, served at alfresco eateries. ◎ *Map M4 • Yurakucho JR tracks • ¥¥*

6 Bangkok Kitchen
Thai restaurant serving green and red curries, northern *laab* salads, and volcanic *tom yam* soups ◎ *Map M5 • Ginza Corridor, 8-2 Saki Ginza, Chuo-ku • 5537-3886 • ¥¥*

7 Sakata
At this popular noodle spot, *sanuki udon*, a thick, buckwheat noodle in a rich broth, is highly regarded. ◎ *Map N4 • 2F, 1-5-13 Ginza, Chuo-ku • 3563-7400 • Closed Sun • ¥*

8 Bird Land
The set meal of skewered *yakitori* features the best free-range birds, chicken liver pate, and grilled breast with Japanese pepper. ◎ *Map M4 • Tsukamoto Sozan Bldg, B1F, 4-2-15 Ginza, Chuo-ku • 5250-1081 • Closed Sun–Mon • ¥¥¥*

9 Enoteca Pinchiorri
This glamorous restaurant serves Toscana and Medici Florentine dishes. There are 150,000-plus bottles stored in the wine cellar. ◎ *Map M4 • Core Bldg, 7F, 5-8-20 Ginza, Chuo-ku • 3289-8081 • ¥¥¥¥*

10 Ohmatsuya
Gourmet fare from rural Yamagata prefecture includes charcoal-grilled meats, fish, and mountain vegetables. ◎ *Map M4 • Ail d'Oro Bldg, 2F, 6-5-8 Ginza, Chuo-ku • 3571-7053 • Closed Sun • ¥¥¥*

Following pages **Fireworks over Sumida River**

Left **Old graves, Yanaka Cemetery** Right **Edo-Shitamachi Traditional Crafts Museum**

Ueno, Asakusa, and Yanaka

THE PARTIAL MODERNIZATION of Tokyo's older quarters to the northeast has not altered their character and flavor. Although gritty, picturesque Ueno is home to museums, temples, and a cherry-filled park. Dotted with religious sites and traditional restaurants, Asakusa appeals as much to the hedonist as the Buddhist acolyte. With its narrow lanes, old wooden houses, craft stores, sanctuaries, and a mossy cemetery, Yanaka is the best preserved of the three old districts.

🔟 Sights

1 Ueno Park
2 National Science Museum
3 Tokyo Metropolitan Art Museum
4 Tokyo National Museum
5 Taikan Yokoyama Memorial Hall
6 Senso-ji Temple
7 Edo-Shitamachi Traditional Crafts Museum
8 Hanayashiki
9 Kappabashi Kitchenware Town
10 Yanaka Cemetery

Ornate exterior of the Senso-ji Temple

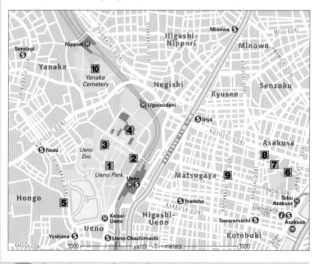

Preceding pages **Sumida River fireworks**

Acrobats performing in Ueno Park

Ueno Park
This wonderful park is an engaging mix of leisure and culture. Among the highlights are the Tokyo National Museum, with the world's largest collection of Japanese arts and antiquities, contemporary and Western art and science museums, avenues of cherry trees, and the Toshogu Shrine – a fine historical monument. More leisure-orientated are its restaurants, cafés, zoo, and a huge pond divided into a boating area, conservation corner, and a magnificent lotus pond (see pp16–17).

National Science Museum
A giant whale model outside the building announces this enormous museum, which is divided into the original, recently renovated section and a newer annex. Older displays and exhibits of dinosaurs, asteroids, fossils, and a reconstructed house made from mammoth tusks vie with touchscreen panels, video displays, and models. ❧ Map F1 • 7-20 Ueno Koen, Taito-ku • 3822-0111 • Open 9am–5pm Tue–Thu, 9am–8pm Fri, 9am–5pm Sat–Sun • Adm

Tokyo Metropolitan Art Museum
The sunken, partially underground floors of the redbrick building designed by architect Maekawa Kunio may not be the perfect place to present art, but the contents are always interesting. The main hall shows an eclectic mix, ranging from Japanese flower arrangements and ink-brush works, to contemporary installations. The art library is first-rate. ❧ Map F1 • 8-36 Ueno Koen, Taito-ku • 3823-6921 • Open 9am–5pm Tue–Sun • Adm • www.tobikan.jp

Tokyo National Museum
This acclaimed museum is the centerpiece of Ueno Park. The Honkan, the main gallery, has a permanent collection of Japanese arts and archeological displays. The Toyokan features arts and crafts from Asia, with a strong Chinese, Central Asian, and Korean showing. The Heiseikan shows archeological objects. The cool, ultra-modern glass lines of the Gallery of Horyu-ji Treasures contrast with its permanent collection of precious religious artifacts. The Hokeikan is a hall used for educational and special exhibits. The building is a fine example of solidly Occidental, Meiji-era architecture (see pp18–19).

Whale sculpture, National Science Museum

The English signs at the National Science Museum are adequate, but for more detail rent an English-language audio guide.

Around Town – Ueno, Asakusa, and Yanaka

Rickshaws

The *jinrikisha* was invented in Japan in 1869. Izumi Yosuke's workshop produced the prototype, a great transportation innovation in Tokyo's narrow roads and rough surfaces. Four years later, there were over 34,000 registered rickshaws in the city, continuing to be a common sight until WWII. Beautifully lacquered rickshaws have made a comeback in tourist spots such as Asakusa. Expect to pay ¥5,000 for a 15-minute ride.

5 Taikan Yokoyama Memorial Hall

Taikan Yokoyama (1868–1958) was a master of Nihonga, a style of painting that fused nativist themes and traditional materials with modern art techniques. A giant among modern Japanese painters, Yokoyama lived in this house for almost 90 years, witnessing immense changes in both the country and its arts. His works are diplayed inside the house, located just opposite Shinobazu Pond. ◈ *Map F2*
• *1-4-24 Ikenohata, Taito-ku* • *3821-1017*

6 Senso-ji Temple

Tokyo's mother temple looms majestically at the end of Nakamise, an avenue of stores selling iconic trinkets. Two imposing gates lead to the great

incense burner standing before the cavernous main hall, designed in a style known as *gongen-zukuri*. Within the same compound, Asakusa Shrine was founded in 1649 and rebuilt several times. Erected even earlier, the nearby 1618 Nitenmon gate remains completely intact, a miraculous survivor of earthquakes, typhoons, and air raids *(see pp10–11)*.

7 Edo-Shitamachi Traditional Crafts Museum

Also known as Gallery Takumi, this museum was set up to preserve and promote local craft industries and techniques dating from the Edo period. More than 300 displays represent 50 different traditional crafts. Craft demonstrations take place on weekends. ◈ *Map R1* • *2-22-13 Asakusa, Taito-ku* • *3842-1990* • *Open 10am–8pm*

8 Hanayashiki

Once part of an aristocratic residence to the west of Senso-ji Temple, the Hanayashiki gardens were opened in 1853 in the Asakusa Rokku entertainment district. A small zoo was added 20 years later. An Asakusa institution, it retains its retro quality, with old-fashioned game machines that complement an

Old-fashioned attractions inside Hanayashiki Amusement Park

 The must-see Senso-ji Temple is the site of the annual spring Sanja Matsuri, one of Tokyo's greatest festivals.

eerily realistic ghost house dating from the 1950s, and Japan's oldest rollercoaster. 🔊 *Map R1* • *2-28-1 Asakusa, Taito-ku* • *3842-8780* • *Open 10am–6pm Mon, Wed–Sun* • *Adm*

Items for sale, Kappabashi Kitchenware Town

9 Kappabashi Kitchenware Town

A long street, Kappabashi-dori is known by its sobriquet, "Kitchen Town." Two stores, Maizuru and Biken, are highly rated by connoisseurs of plastic food. Food samples have generated interest as a minor, collectable pop art. Viewed on an empty stomach, they can seem like works of towering genius. 🔊 *Map Q2* • *Kappabashi-dori, Taito-ku*

10 Yanaka Cemetery

Explore this city of the dead in the mossy folds of Yanaka, an endearingly unfashionable quarter. Among the tombs and worn statues of Buddhist deities and bodhisattvas are the gravestones of authors, statesmen, philosophers, actors, Japan's last shogun, and those who committed crimes that caught the popular imagination. Oden Takahashi, a woman who massacred men, lies here unrepentant *(see pp26–7)*.

A Day in Old Asakusa

⟮ Morning ⟯

Exit Asakusa subway, walk north along Umamichi-dori until you reach Kototoi-dori. Turn left and the **Edo-Shitamachi Traditional Crafts Museum** is a short walk away. The nearby **Hanayashiki Amusement Park** is a relic of the old entertainment district of Rokku. Immediately south, **Asakusa Kannon Onsen** is a traditional hot spring. Just west of the baths, the Rokku Broadway pedestrian street still boasts a few traditional theaters, comedy and story-telling halls, including the **Asakusa Engei Hall**. Stop to look at the posters and lively barkers outside. The narrow backstreets around **Denboin-dori** have many cheap, but characterful, restaurants serving fried noodles and *oden*, a fish-cake hot pot.

⟮ Afternoon ⟯

Walk south to the great **Kaminari-mon**, the main entrance to Senso-ji Temple, to admire the giant paper lantern and the ancient guardian devils. Walk toward the Sumida River and the station where you began, turn right on Edo-dori for **Gallery ef**, housed in an earth-walled, 19th-century storehouse, a rarity in contemporary Tokyo. The café here is excellent. Retrace your steps to the station area and stop at the brightly painted **Azumabashi Bridge**, where traditional pleasure boats, *yakata-bune*, are moored. Return to the corner of Kaminari-mon and Umamichi streets to visit the **Kamiya Bar** *(see p42)*, another Asakusa institution, for *denki-bran*, their trademark drink.

The English-speaking staff at the Asakusa Culture and Sightseeing Center, opposite the Kaminari-mon gate, provide maps.

85

Left **Stone lanterns, Yanaka Cemetery** Center **Isetatsu** Right **Tenno-ji Temple**

🔟 Top 10 Yanaka Sights

1 Suwa Shrine
During the New Year, the grounds of this 1322 shrine on the edge of a plateau are strung with lanterns showing the zodiac sign for the coming year. ⓢ *Map F1 • Yanaka, Taito-ku*

2 Joko-ji Temple
Buddhist statues stand near the entrance to this shrine, also known as the "Snow-Viewing Temple," a popular location during the Edo era for watching snow-flakes. ⓢ *Map F1 • Yanaka, Taito-ku*

3 Asakura Choso Museum
The home and studio of sculptor Fumio Asakura (1883–1964) contains statues of famous people. ⓢ *Map F1 • 7-18-10 Yanaka, Taito-ku • 3821-4549 • Open 9:30am–4:30pm Tue–Thu, Sat, Sun • Adm*

4 Yanaka Cemetery
Many famous Japanese people are interred in this cemetery set up in 1874 (see pp26–7).

5 Tenno-ji temple
Founded in 1274, this temple contains the Great Buddha of Yanaka, a fine bronze statue cast in 1690. ⓢ *Map F1 • Yanaka, Taito-ku*

6 Gamo Residence
This well-restored, Meiji-era merchant house exemplifies a *dashigeta-zukuri* structure, where wooden beams extend out from the upper levels of the building. ⓢ *Map F1 • Yanaka, Taito-ku*

7 Zensho-an Temple
The main hall of the temple, a venue for Zen meditation, is dwarfed by a 20-ft (6-m) statue of the goddess Kannon. The fine 1991 figure is covered in gold leaf. ⓢ *Map F1 • Yanaka, Taito-ku*

8 Daien-ji Temple
This interesting temple has a Buddhist and a Shinto hall. A Chrysanthemum Festival, with dolls made from flowers, is held here annually on October 14–15. ⓢ *Map F1 • Yanaka, Taito-ku*

9 Isetatsu
This 1864 shop creates *chiyogami* – patterned *washi* paper once popular with the samurai class. ⓢ *Map F1 • 2-18-9 Yanaka, Taito-ku • 3823-1453*

10 Daimyo Clock Museum
This museum is dedicated to timepieces made for the privileged classes during the Edo era. Instead of numerals, the 12 signs of the Chinese zodiac were used to indicate the hour. ⓢ *Map F1 • 2-11-27 Yanaka, Taito-ku • 3821-6913 • Open 10am–4pm Tue–Sun • Adm*

One of the main highlights of the Asakura Choso Museum is its intriguing garden, the Water Garden of Five Percepts.

Price Categories

Price ranges are for an average-size dinner for one. Lunchtime menus are often less expensive.	¥ Under ¥2,000
	¥¥ ¥2,000–¥5,000
	¥¥¥ ¥5,000–¥10,000
	¥¥¥¥ Over ¥10,000

Delicacies served at Asakusa Imahan

Top 10 Restaurants

1 Sasanoyuki
Famed for its silky tofu dishes, this acclaimed restaurant has been around since the Edo period. ◎ *Map G1* • *2-15-10 Negishi, Taito-ku* • *3873-1145* • *Closed Mon* • *¥¥*

2 Sometaro
The only dish here is *okonomiyaki*, pancakes made with shrimp, octopus, and vegetables. ◎ *Map Q2* • *2-2-2 Nishi-Asakusa, Taito-ku* • *3844-9502*

3 Namiki Yabu Soba
This ever-popular *soba* (buckwheat noodle) shop is located near the Senso-ji temple. ◎ *Map R2* • *2-11-9 Kaminarimon, Taito-ku* • *3841-1340* • *Closed Sun* • *¥*

4 Hantei
Housed in a magnificent Meiji-era building, this place serves *kushiage*, deep-fried skewers of delicately prepared meat, fish, and vegetables. ◎ *Map F1* • *2-12-15 Nezu, Bunkyo-ku* • *3828-1440* • *Closed Mon* • *¥¥*

5 Nezu Club
Refined Japanese cuisine in an informal setting. Ordering the set dinner is the easiest approach. ◎ *Map F1* • *2-30-2 Nezu, Bunkyo-ku* • *3828-4004* • *Closed Sun–Tue* • *¥¥¥*

6 Daikokuya
Expect long lines for the delicious fish and vegetable tempura dishes at this popular eatery. ◎ *Map R2* • *1-38-10 Asakusa, Taito-ku* • *3844-1111* • *Closed Sun* • *¥¥*

7 Ikenohata Yabu Soba
This branch of a popular *soba* chain serves classic noodles in a thick broth. The cold summer soba also appeals to many Japanese customers. ◎ *Map F2* • *3-44-7 Yushima, Bunkyo-ku* • *3831-8977* • *Closed Wed* • *¥*

8 Komagata Dojo
Grilled and stewed loach, a fish resembling a freshwater sardine, is served in this 200-year-old restaurant. ◎ *Map R2* • *1-7-12 Komagata, Taito-ku* • *3842-4001* • *¥*

9 Asakusa Imahan
Shabu-shabu consists of wafer-thin prime cuts of beef dipped and blanched in a boiling broth at your table; served with vegetables and rice. ◎ *Map Q2* • *2-2-5 Nishi-Asakusa, Taito-ku* • *3841-2690* • *¥¥*

10 Saboh Hanahenro
A two-floor teahouse with green tea, coffee, and home-made cakes. Their tasty lunch boxes sell out quickly. ◎ *Map F1* • *7-17-11 Yanaka, Taito-ku* • *3822-6387* • *¥ (lunch box)*

Left **Zojo-ji Temple** Right **San-mon Gate**

Roppongi and Akasaka

ONE OF TOKYO'S PREMIER NIGHTLIFE DISTRICTS, *Roppongi is a major center for the arts, shopping, communications, and lifestyle. The opening of Roppongi Hills, a multicomplex mini-city, inspired the building of several other modern, innovative centers and facilities, including the more recent Tokyo Midtown. Its art pretensions have not detracted from its reputation as one of the liveliest nightspots in town, with upscale restaurants, pubs, bars, and*

music and dance clubs. Akasaka looks contemporary, but is more of an establishment area, where political deals are still brokered in the rarefied air of chic restaurants and hotels. It also has some of Tokyo's most revered temples and shrines.

National Art Center Tokyo

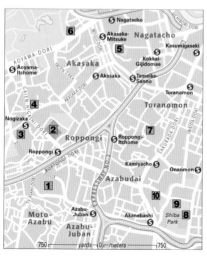

Sights

1. Roppongi Hills
2. Tokyo Midtown
3. Nogi Shrine
4. National Art Center Tokyo
5. Hie Shrine
6. Toyokawa Inari Shrine and Temple
7. Musee Tomo
8. San-mon Gate
9. Zojo-ji Temple
10. Tokyo Tower

1 Roppongi Hills
Completed in 2003, this sprawling city-within-a-city includes gardens and a live-performance area. The central structure, the 54-story Mori Tower, houses some of the world's largest companies, more than 200 stores, restaurants, bars, and the Grand Hyatt Hotel. The Mori Art Museum, on the 52nd and 53rd floors, is one of Tokyo's most innovative art venues. ◎ Map C6 • 6-10 Roppongi, Minato-ku • 6406-6000 • www.roppongihills.com

2 Tokyo Midtown
Unveiled in 2007, Tokyo Midtown sets aside 40 percent of the complex for the landscaped Hinokicho Park and Midtown Garden. Midtown Tower, the tallest building in Tokyo, and its core of buildings contain offices, apartments, high-end fashion stores, restaurants, cafés, bars, and the Ritz-Carlton Tokyo hotel. The site's cultural credentials are enhanced by the presence of the fascinating Suntory Museum of Art and 21_21 Design Sight, a design gallery conceived by architect Ando Tadao and fashion guru Issey Miyake. ◎ Map C6 • Akasaka, Minato-ku • 3475-3100 • www.tokyo-midtown.com

Sparse interior of the Nogi Shrine

3 Nogi Shrine
This modest but significant shrine honors General Nogi Meresuke, who, along with his wife, committed ritual suicide in an act of loyalty when the Meiji emperor died on September 13, 1912. The event divided the country into those who admired the act as a heroic gesture, and those who condemned it as an archaic practice. The general's house stands beside the shrine, and is open only on the eve of the couple's death. ◎ Map C5 • 8-11-27 Akasaka, Minato-ku • 3478-3001

4 National Art Center Tokyo
Japan's largest exhibition space, the center hosts temporary exhibitions, such as Nitten, a prestigious annual event highlighting Japanese and Western painting, sculpture, craftwork, and calligraphy. The 2007 building is a wonder to behold, with its undulating glass façade, slated walls, and natural wood floor. ◎ Map C6 • 7-22-2 Roppongi, Minato-ku • 6812-9900 • Open 10am–6pm Wed–Thu, Sat–Sun; 10am–8pm Fri • Adm • www.nact.jp

Towering buildings, Tokyo Midtown

 The admission ticket for the Mori Art Museum entitles visitors to enjoy the Tokyo City View and Café panoramas.

Hie Shrine, one of Tokyo's revered temples

Hie Shrine

Burned down in the air raids of 1945 and rebuilt in 1967, the Hie Shrine was originally erected as a protective shrine. Its role of deflecting evil spirits from Edo Castle still echoes in wood carvings to the left of the main shrine, depicting a monkey protectively cradling a baby. Pregnant women still come here to pray for safe deliveries. The biannual Sanno Matsuri, one of Tokyo's great festivals, puts the shrine firmly on the city's cultural map. ⊗ Map J4 • 2-10-5 Nagatacho, Chiyoda-ku • 3581-2471

Toyokawa Inari Shrine and Temple

A Zen temple with some Shinto elements, the shrine has an interesting approach, lined with orange banners, lanterns, and statues of foxes, the bodhisattva Jizo (protector of children and travelers), and Kannon, (the Goddess of Mercy). Behind the main buildings are forest-like paths lined with *senbon nobori* streamers hung by devotees in the hope of fulfilling their wishes. Small eateries inside the shrine serve tasty *oden* (fish cake stew) and *kitsune soba* (buckwheat noodles and fried tofu). ⊗ Map D5 • 1-4-7 Moto-Azabu, Minato-ku • 3408-3414

Toyokawa Inari Shrine and Temple

Musee Tomo

Established in 2003 by Tomo Kikuchi, a collector of contemporary ceramics, this small museum is one of the most elegant in Tokyo. Exhibitions change every few months, highlighting a particular craftsperson or a school of ceramic ware, such as Bizen or Raku. ⊗ Map K5 • 4-1-35 Toranomon, Minato-ku • 5733-5311 • Open 11am–6pm Tue–Sun • Adm

San-mon Gate

Fires and earthquakes have been reducing Tokyo's buildings to rubble for over 400 years, but the San-mon Gate, the main entrance to Zojo-ji Temple, has remained miraculously intact. The oldest wooden structure in the city, it was erected in 1605. The three tiers of the red-lacquered gate, an Important Cultural Treasure, represent the three stages required to enter Nirvana.

Roppongi Street Art

Many world-class artists were asked to create works on and around Roppongi Hills. Louise Bourgeois's huge spider sculpture, *Maman,* is the most visible, but there are also wall drawings, a lit-up robot, a giant coffee bean installation, digital screen models, a 3-D landscape painting, and waveform furniture such as interesting benches.

The gate looks awesome at night, when it is illuminated.
🗺 Map E6 • Shiba-koen, Minato-ku

9 Zojo-ji Temple

Another victim of WWII air raids, the temple is a 1970s ferro-concrete reconstruction. The original temple was founded in 1393 and then removed to its present location in 1598. In the next century, it was chosen by the Tokugawa shoguns as their ancestral temple. Today, it hosts many religious events. The main hall contains ancient statues, sutras, and other sacred objects.
🗺 Map E6 • Shiba-koen, Minato-ku
• 3432-1431 • Open 6am–5:30pm

Tokyo Tower etched against a clear sky

10 Tokyo Tower

When it was opened in 1958 as a broadcasting mast, this Eiffel Tower clone was the tallest building in Tokyo. Despite its shabby aquarium, trick art museum, tacky waxworks, and souvenir stores, it attracts a large number of visitors spurred by nostalgia and the popularity of a 2007 film of the same name.
🗺 Map K6 • 4-2-8 Shiba-koen, Minato-ku
• 3433-5111 • Open 9am–10pm

A Day in the Art Triangle

Morning

🕐 Exiting Roppongi-Ichome subway, the informative **Okura Shukokan Museum of Fine Art** is a five-minute stroll away. The museum opens at 10am, but is closed on Mondays. You cannot miss this Chinese-style building, directly across from the stylish Hotel Okura, perfect for a coffee break. A ten-minute walk away is Roppongi Hills and its centerpiece, the **Mori Art Museum**, with its superb Tokyo City View observation deck. Cross Roppongi-dori and walk north to the **National Art Center**, a huge 12-room art venue where you can lunch at **Brasserie Paul Bocuse Le Musée** (see p93) with views of the Roppongi skyline. Descend to the Center for an eclectic mix of art, displayed regularly in its temporary shows.

Afternoon

Heading north in the direction of Nogi Shrine, visit **Gallery Ma** (see p39). Sponsored by the bathroom appliance and fixtures company, Toto, it focuses mainly on architecture. A great place to experience the latest trends in the Tokyo design world, and see the work of foreign architects, the gallery also has an excellent bookstore. A short walk south from here is Tokyo Midtown.

Vinoteca is an exceptional wine bar on the second floor of the Garden Terrace. To reach your table, you walk through a tunnel with wine bottles displayed behind plexiglass panels on the walls, ceiling, and floor.

Around Town – Roppongi and Akasaka

Left **Gas Panic** Center **Mado Lounge** Right **Tokyo Sports Café**

Top 10 Clubs and Bars

1 Core
Techno and house reign here, but there are plenty of other sounds in this eclectic club. ✪ Map C6 • TSK CCC Bldg, B1-2F, 7-15-30 Roppongi, Minato-ku • 3470-5944 • Closed Mon–Tue • Adm

2 Y2K
For a decade, this club has been promoting live rock bands, including newcomers. ✪ Map C6 • Aban Bldg, B1F, 7-13-2 Roppongi, Minato-ku • 5775-3676 • Closed Mon • Adm

3 Tokyo Sports Café
Tokyo's largest sports café keeps late hours so you can catch live international games on its two screens. ✪ Map C6 • Fusion Bldg, 2F, 7-13-8 Roppongi, Minato-ku • 5411-8939 • Closed Sun

4 Agave Clover
If the cantina decor doesn't tell you this expensive drinking hole is a Mexican bar, the 400 varieties of tequila will. ✪ Map C6 • Clover Bldg, 2F, 7-15-10 Roppongi, Minato-ku • 3497-0229 • Closed Sun

5 Gas Panic
Popular with expatriates, the three bars offer drinks at afford-able prices. ✪ Map J6 • 2-3F, 3-15-24 Roppongi, Minato-ku • 3405-0633

6 Paddy Foley's Irish Pub
One of Tokyo's first Irish pubs, this place is popular with locals and expatriates. ✪ Map D6 • Roi Bldg, B1F, 5-5-1 Roppongi, Minato-ku • 3423-2250

7 Alfie
This jazz club is a complete world of entertainment, with a big dance floor, café, restaurant, and lounge all on different levels. ✪ Map D6 • Hama Roppongi Bldg, 5F, 6-2-35 Roppongi, Minato-ku • 3479-2037 • Closed Sun

8 Salsa Sudada
Tokyo's salsa boom shows no sign of slowing. This place also features mambo and rumba. ✪ Map C6 • 3F, 7-13-8 Roppongi, Minato-ku • 5474-8806 • Adm

9 Cavern Club
Tokyo's ultimate tribute band plays the Fab Four's song catalog with astonishing finesse. Beatles requests are welcome. ✪ Map D6 • Saito Bldg, 1F, 5-3-2 Roppongi, Minato-ku • 3405-5207 • Adm

10 Mado Lounge
Mellow DJ music, drinks, and the intergalactic heights create magic here. The club is integrated into Roppongi Hill's Tokyo City View observatory. ✪ Map C6 • Mori Tower, 52F, 6-10-1 Roppongi, Minato-ku • 03-3470-0052 • Closed Sun • Adm

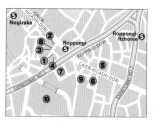

The entrance fee to Mado Lounge also allows a visit to the Mori Art Museum.

Price Categories

Price ranges are for an average-size dinner for one. Lunchtime menus are often less expensive.

¥	Under ¥2,000
¥¥	¥2,000–¥5,000
¥¥¥	¥5,000–¥10,000
¥¥¥¥	Over ¥10,000

Sophisticated interior of Sicilia restaurant

📷 Top 10 Places to Eat

1 Mikawa
The specialty here is Edo-period "Edomae" tempura. ◈ Map C6 • Roppongi Hills Residence B, 6-12-2 Roppongi, Minato-ku • 3423-8100 • Closed Wed • ¥¥¥

2 Pintokono
At this conveyor-belt sushi bar, serve yourself, or bellow out your orders for even fresher fish. ◈ Map C6 • Hollywood Plaza, B2F, B2F, 6-4-1 Roppongi, Minato-ku • 5771-1133 • ¥¥

3 Fukuzushi
Beside the usual tuna and squid offerings are the less common shad, conger eel, and other delicacies at this no-frills sushi restaurant. ◈ Map D6 • 5-7-8 Roppongi, Minato-ku • 3402-4116 • ¥¥¥

4 Inakaya
An old-fashioned *robatayaki* (grilled food) eatery, offering all manner of meat and other foods. ◈ Map J6 • 5-3-4 Roppongi, Minato-ku • 3408-5040 • ¥¥¥¥

5 Nodaiwa
Specializing in wild eel, Nodaiwa serves charcoal-grilled fish drizzled with an appetizing sauce. ◈ Map J6 • 1-5-4 Higashi-Azabu, Minato-ku • 3583-7852 • Closed Sun • ¥¥

6 Hassan
The star course here is the set, all-you-can-eat dinner of *shabu-shabu*, thin strips of high-quality beef dipped in boiling broth. ◈ Map D6 • Denki Bldg, B1, 6-1-20 Roppongi, Minato-ku • 3403-8333 • ¥¥¥

7 Ukai Tofuya
Countless variations of expertly prepared *tofu* are served in mini-dishes. A lovely Japanese garden setting beyond the windows. ◈ Map K6 • 4-4-13 Shiba Koen, Minato-ku • 3436-1028 • ¥¥¥

8 Sicilia
Mouthwatering pizzas and salads are served here at unbeatable prices for Roppongi. It can get very busy on week-ends, though. ◈ Map D6 • B1F, 6-1-26 Roppongi, Minato-ku • 3405-4653 • ¥

9 Brasserie Paul Bocuse Le Musée
Located inside the striking National Arts Center building, this stylish restaurant serves light French cuisine. Fixed-price lunches draw a huge crowd. ◈ Map C6 • 3F National Arts Center, 7-22-2 Roppongi, Minato-ku • 5770-8161 • ¥¥¥

10 Erawan
A classy Thai restaurant with a beautiful teakwood interior. Spicy dishes and Thai staff add to the authenticity. ◈ Map D6 • Roi Bldg, 13F, 5-5-1 Roppongi, Minato-ku • 3404-5741 • ¥¥¥

Around Town – Roppongi and Akasaka

Left **Parco Museum of Art and Beyond** Right **Tepco Electric Energy Museum**

Aoyama, Omotesando, Harajuku, and Shibuya

OMOTESANDO-DORI, THE CHIC BOULEVARD running through Aoyama and Omotesando, is Tokyo's fashion quarter. A shift in mood occurs as Omotesando segues into Harajuku and Takeshita-dori, a street humming with off-the-peg boutiques, street stalls, fast-food joints, and a young crowd. Giant video screens characterize Shibuya, which is lined with fashion and department stores, music clubs, museums, art galleries, and cafés.

Yoyogi National Stadium

Sights

1. Spiral
2. Nezu Institute of Fine Arts
3. Ukiyo-e Ota Memorial Museum of Art
4. Takeshita-dori and Togo Shrine
5. Yoyogi National Stadium
6. Bunkamura
7. Toguri Museum of Art
8. Meiji Shrine
9. Parco Museum of Art and Beyond
10. Tepco Electric Energy Museum

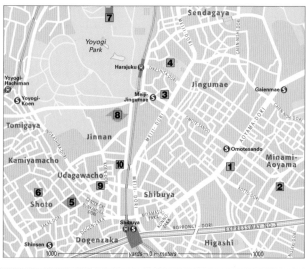

Curving ramp at Spiral

1 Spiral
Tasked with creating a space that would combine music, the visual arts, theater, a restaurant, bar and café with an exciting architectural concept, designer Fumihiko Maki came up with the idea of a spiral. The shape, standing for the idea of cultural flow, is replicated on both the inside and outside of the building. A curving ramp takes visitors up to the main gallery, where art-, design- and fashion-related shows take place. ⊗ *Map B6* • *5-6-23 Minami-Aoyama, Minato-ku* • *34998-1171* • *Open 11am–8pm*

2 Nezu Institute of Fine Arts
Concealed behind sandstone walls, this museum was established by the Meiji-era tycoon and politician Kaichiro Nezu. Some of the collection's textiles, laquer-ware, and ceramics are so rare that they are registered as National Treasures. The most famous piece is Ogata Korin's screen painting, *Irises.* ⊗ *Map C6* • *6-5-1 Minami-Aoyama, Minato-ku* • *3400-2536* • *Open 9:30am–4:30pm Tue–Sun* • *Adm* • *www. nezu-muse.or.jp*

3 Ukiyo-e Ota Memorial Museum of Art
This remarkable museum has Tokyo's finest collection of *ukiyo-e* woodblock prints – a whopping 12,000 in all. The great names in this genre, such as Harunobu, Utamaru, Hokusai, and Sharaku, are all featured here. The collection was begun by Seizo Ota, a wealthy businessman who realized that many of the best works were being sold to foreign museums. ⊗ *Map B5* • *1-10-10 Jingumae, Shibuya-ku* • *3403-0880* • *Open 10:30am–5:30pm Tue–Sun* • *Adm*

4 Takeshita-dori and Togo Shrine
On a weekend, narrow Takeshita street is probably the single-most crowded spot in the entire city. The home of subculture kitsch, the street is packed with theme clothing stores, takeout food, crepe stands, and stores selling character items, cuddly toys, and accessories. Just a few steps behind the street are the serenely quiet precincts of the Togo Shrine. Dedicated to Admiral Heihachiro Togo, who engineered the defeat of the Russian fleet in 1905, the grounds are a great escape from the heaving mass of Takeshita-dori. On the first and fourth Sundays of the month, an excellent flea market is held here. ⊗ *Map B5* • *Harajuku, Minato-ku*

A street scene in busy Takeshita-dori

The Nezu Institute of Fine Arts has a lovely garden full of trees, Buddha statues, and elegant tea pavilions.

Aoyama Playtime

Aoyama is not all serious shopping and galleries, as you will realise when you glimpse the hydra-headed sculpture outside the National Children's Castle *(see p60)*. This delightful work of art was created by Taro Okamoto. The castle itself is a four-floor wonderland of playhouses, climbing frames, hands-on music, computer and painting rooms, and a fabulous rooftop play port, replete with jungle gyms, tunnels, unicycles, and go-carts.

Yoyogi National Stadium

A residential compound for American personnel during the Occupation (1945–52), the park area was called "Washington Heights." The Japanese government requested its return, turning the site into the Olympic Village in 1964 when Tokyo hosted the Games. Architect Tange Kenzo designed the Olympic pavilions, erected at the park's southern end. The sweeping roofs of the pavilions still look very contemporary. ◈ *Map R4 • 2-1-1 Jinnan, Shibuya-ku • 3468-1171*

Bunkamura

Bunkamura, "Culture Village" in Japanese, is Shibuya's foremost art and theater venue. This multicomplex center houses the Bunkamura Museum of Art, Bunkamura Gallery, the Orchard Hall (a small but world-class venue for music, opera, and ballet) and the Theater Cocoon (an art cinema). Exhibitions include big name artists and photographers, from Monet to Henri Cartier-Bresson. A branch of the famous Paris café, Les Deux Magots, is here. ◈ *Map Q5 • 2-24-1 Dogenzaka, Shibuya-ku • 3477-9111 • Open 10am–7pm Mon–Thu, Sun; 10am–9pm Fri–Sat • www.bunkamura.co.jp*

Toguri Museum of Art

This small museum in a leafy residential area has an outstanding collection of Oriental porcelain. The Japanese collection includes fine examples of Imari and Nabeshima ware, the Chinese pieces represent the Tang, Song, and later dynasties. The highlight of the Korean section are fine Koryo-era pieces. ◈ *Map Q5 • 1-11-3 Shoto, Shibuya-ku • 3465-0070 • Open 9:30am–5:30pm Tue–Sun • Adm • www.toguri-museum.or.jp*

Meiji Shrine

A massive gate marks the entrance to the forested compound and outer grounds of the Meiji Shrine. Broadleaf trees and shrubs are planted beside gravel paths leading to the shrine. Burned to cinders in WWII, the

The impressive interior of the Theater Cocoon in Bunkamura's cultural multiplex

Four annual shows rotate the large collection of Toguri Museum of Art, though only a fraction of the exhibits are displayed each year.

The main gate leading to Meiji Shrine

current 1958 building is a
faithful reproduction of the
original shrine dedicated to
the Meiji Emperor, who died
in 1912 *(see pp24–5)*.

9 Parco Museum of Art and Beyond

Bold pop-culture exhibitions run
throughout the year at this gallery, which contains three main
spaces: the Logos Gallery, Parco
Factory, and The Other Space.
Renowned, unknown, and
notorious Japanese and foreign
artists, photographers, and print
and graphic designers are pre-
sented in the shows here. ⊗ *Map
R5 • Parco Part 3, 7F, 15-1 Udagawacho,
Shibuya-ku • 3496-1287 • Open 10am–
9pm • Adm • www.parco-art.com*

10 Tepco Electric Energy Museum

A big hit with kids, this
seven-story museum dedicated
to electricity has plenty for
adults too. There are several
hands-on displays here. The
fourth floor takes visitors into
the home of a typical Japanese
family, examining the electrical
circuitry. There is an English-
language pamphlet at the
entrance. ⊗ *Map R4 • 1-12-10 Jinnan,
Shibuya-ku • 3477-1191 • Open 10am–
6pm Mon, Tue, Thu–Sun*

A Day of Architecture

Morning

🕐 After exiting Omotesando
subway, stroll down
Aoyama-dori until you see
the open plaza outside the
United Nations University
building on your right. The
stately building was created by Tange Kenzo. Turn
back the way you came
until you glimpse **Spiral**
(see p95) on the right.
Return to the intersection
at the subway, and follow
the road on the right until
you see the triangular outline of **Prada Aoyama**,
designed by a famous
Swiss firm. A little farther
on, **Collezione** is the work
of the self-taught architect,
Ando Tadao. Return to the
subway area and the **Hanai
Mori Building**, another
Kenzo Tango design, on
Omotesando-dori. Cross
the road and head to
Maisen restaurant *(see
p99)*. This former traditional
bathhouse now specializes
in *tonkatsu* (pork cutlets).

Afternoon

Back on Omotesando-dori,
heading toward Harajuku,
the leather goods store
Tods, designed by Toyo
Ito, is a fine example of
retail architecture. Across
the road, the **Omotesando
Hills** is a fashion brand
complex with cool lines
and angles. Continue along
the road until you reach
Meiji-dori, then take a left.
A little farther on, you can
see the glass sections and
counter-angles of the 2008
Audi Forum Tokyo. Walk
on to Shibuya station and
the area south of the
tracks, where Makoto Sei
Watanabe's **Aoyama
Technical College** looms
like a malignant sci-fi
machine. Recover from the
shock at **Segafredo**, an
excellent Italian-style café.

Left **Laforet Harajuku** Center **Issey Miyake** Right **Prada Aoyama**

Fashion and Design Hangouts

1 Anniversaire Café
A terrace seat here doesn't come cheap, but this chic café is the place to see and be seen. ⬡ Map B6 • 3-5-30 Kita-Aoyama, Minato-ku • 5411-5988

2 A Bathing Ape
One of Tokyo's most original fashion stores. The distinctive jeans and hoodies attract a very cool, discerning crowd. ⬡ Map S4 • 5-5-8 Minami-Aoyama, Minato-ku • 3407-2145

3 Comme des Garçons
Curving glass windows and tilted walls hint at the creative approach to fashion here at Rei Kawakubo's main fashion store. ⬡ Map B6 • 5-2-1 Minami-Aoyama, Minato-ku • 3406-3951

4 Undercover
The brainchild of former punk musician Jun Takahashi, this store sells youth streetwear. ⬡ Map C6 • Unimat Bleu Cinq Point Bldg, 5-3-18 Minami-Aoyama, Minato-ku

5 Prada Aoyama
Prada's quality, chic offerings are almost overshadowed by the brilliance of the crystal building. ⬡ Map C6 • 5-2-6 Minami-Aoyama, Minato-ku • 0120-559-914

6 Issey Miyake
Original designs, including Miyake's signature single garment pieces, are on display. ⬡ Map B6 • 3-18-11 Minami-Aoyama, Minato-ku • 3423-1407

7 Omotesando Hills
Boutiques, such as Jimmy Choo, and specialist stores, including jewelry e.m., vie with dozens of brand stores here. ⬡ Map B5 • 4-12-10 Jingumae, Shibuya-ku • 3497-0310

8 Cat Street
Designers, such as Todd Oldman, Armani Casa, and Anna Sui, find a home along this fashion road. Cafés and art spaces add to the contemporary blend. ⬡ Map B5 • Omotesando, Minato-ku

9 Laforet Harajuku
The oddball styles offered by hundreds of clothes and accessory stores here attract teens. A great place to observe Tokyo youth and fashion fads. ⬡ Map B5 • 1-11-6 Jingumae, Shibuya-ku • 3475-0411

10 109 Building
From cutting edge to extreme, with a clientele rarely over 20, the clothes sold inside this cylindrical-shaped building are a measure of tomorrow's fashion trends. ⬡ Map R5 • 23-29-1 Dogenzaka, Shibuya-ku • 3477-5111

Price Categories

Price ranges are for an average-size dinner for one. Lunchtime menus are often less expensive.

¥	Under ¥2,000
¥¥	¥2,000–¥5,000
¥¥¥	¥5,000–¥10,000
¥¥¥¥	Over ¥10,000

Bar counter at Las Chicas

Top 10 Places to Eat

1 Natural Harmony Angolo
A non-smoking, mostly vegetarian restaurant with a reputation for very fresh ingredients. ◈ Map B5 • 3-38-12 Jingumae, Shibuya-ku • 3405-8393 • Closed Mon • ¥¥

2 Las Chicas
Simple international and fusion cuisine, wines, and cocktails served by foreign waiters makes Las Chicas a favorite with expats. ◈ Map B6 • 5-47-6 Jingumae, Shibuya-ku • 3407-6865 • Closed Mon • ¥¥

3 Jangara Ramen
Tonkotsu (pork bone) ramen is the best of the Kyushu-style dishes on offer here. ◈ Map B5 • 1-13-21 Jingumae, Shibuya-ku • 3404-5405 • Closed Mon • ¥

4 Gesshinkyo
The chef's original version of Zen vegetarian temple food served here is an eating experience. ◈ Map B5 • 4-24-12 Jingumae, Shibuya-ku • 3796-6575 • Closed Sun • ¥

5 Maisen
Dependable tonkatsu (deep-fried and breaded pork cutlets) are the specialty of this main branch of a well-known chain. ◈ Map B5 • 4-8-5 Jingumae, Shibuya-ku • 3470-0071 • ¥¥

6 Myoko
Try the robust mountain stews made from vegetables, oysters, and kimchee (Korean pickled cabbage). ◈ Map S5 • 1-17-2 Shibuya, Shibuya-ku • 3486-0281 • ¥

7 Fonda de la Madrugada
This authentic Mexican cantina offers enchilladas, stuffed chillies, chicken dishes, and tortillas. ◈ Map B5 • B2F, 2-33-12 Jingumae, Shibuya-ku • 5410-6288 • Closed Mon • ¥¥¥

8 Oh! Calcutta
The Indian fare here includes mutton biryani, spicy chicken, and vegetable curries. Try the ¥1,050-lunch buffet. ◈ Map R5 • Ota Bldg, B1, 26-9 Shibuya, Shibuya-ku • 3780-2315 • ¥¥

9 Mominoki House
Although the dishes are mostly Japanese wholesome vegetarian, there are some departures, such as the venison and fish dishes. ◈ Map B5 • 2-18-5 Jingumae, Shibuya-ku • 3405-9144 • ¥¥

10 Kanetanaka-so
A traditional, very urbane Japanese restaurant serving kaiseki ryori, Japan's seasonally changing and delicate haute cuisine. ◈ Map R6 • Cerulean Tower Tokyu Hotel, 2F, 26-1 Sakuragaoka, Shibuya-ku • 3476-3420 • ¥¥¥¥

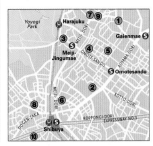

Natural Harmony Angolo also has a natural foods and natural convenience store.

Left **Takashimaya Times Square** Right **Bunka Gakuen Costume Museum**

Shinjuku

RESEMBLING AN ALL-PURPOSE CITY, *Shinjuku is replete with a large garden-park, train stations, shopping complexes, and department stores. Railway lines split the area into two sub-cities. The windy avenues in West Shinjuku are dominated by offices, stores, and experimental skyscrapers. East Shinjuku is a legacy of the 1960s, when the area's Bohemian quarter attracted artists, writers, and political activists. Though cultural features exist on both sides, East Shinjuku appears more hedonistic, with its neon-illuminated nightspots and a sprawling red-light district.*

Sights

1. Bunka Gakuen Costume Museum
2. Sompo Japan Museum of Art
3. Pentax Forum
4. NTT InterCommunication Center
5. Tokyo Metropolitan Government Building
6. Shinjuku Gyoen
7. Kabuki-cho
8. Hanazono Shrine
9. Golden Gai
10. Takashimaya Times Square

Brightly illuminated night scene in Kabuki-cho

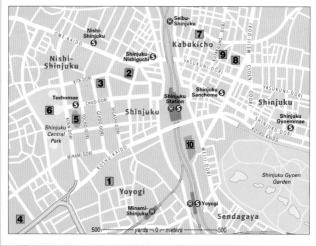

Preceding pages **Rainbow Bridge, Odaiba Island**

Around Town – Shinjuku

1 Bunka Gakuen Costume Museum

This museum is a part of Bunka Women's University, an elite fashion design school. The historical collection, a fraction of which can be shown at a time, ranges from a Heian-era 12-layered kimono to costumes worn by Noh actors.

Pentax Forum, Mitsui Building

More modern designs include the Japanese take on the Swinging Sixties. Scrolls and other illustrations show the types of clothing worn by Japanese people through the ages. ✎ Map A4 • 3-22-7 Yoyogi, Shibuya-ku • 3299-2387 • Open 10am–4:30pm Mon–Sat • Adm

2 Sompo Japan Museum of Art

This museum showcases the works of Togo Seiji (1897–1980), an artist whose images, mainly of women, hover between Art Deco, Cubism, and Japanese animation figures. There are also a number of paintings by European artists such as Gauguin and Cezanne. The insurance company that owns the building made news in the 1980s bubble economy years when it bought Van Gogh's *Sunflowers* for an unheard-of ¥5 billion. ✎ Map A3 • Sompo Japan Bldg, 42F, 1-26-1 Nishi-Shinjuku • 5405-8686 • Open 10am–6pm Tue–Sun • Adm • www.sompo-japan.co.jp/museum

3 Pentax Forum

This photo gallery, camera museum, and service center is located in the Mitsui Building. Besides the exhibitions of world-class photography and displays by gifted amateurs, there is a collection of almost every camera made by Pentax. The hands-on displays allow visitors to try out everything. The forum's goal to "improve the photographic culture" involves new angles on the art of photography through events, lectures, and demonstrations of photo techniques in their Open Studio. ✎ Map A3 • Shinjuku Mitsui Bldg, 1F, 2-1-1 Nishi-Shinjuku, Shinjuku-ku • 3348-2941 • Open 10:30am–6:30pm

4 NTT InterCommunication Center

Part of the Tokyo Opera City office and culture complex, the center holds exhibitions that show the link between technology and creativity. Run by the telecom giant NTT, the permanent and temporary installations, video art, and interactive displays explore this connection between art, media design, and the latest techno wizardry. The excellent video library includes the work of cutting-edge artists, including Laurie Anderson and Nam June Paik. ✎ Map A4 • Tokyo Opera City Tower, 4F, 3-20-2 Nishi-Shinjuku • 0120-144-199 • Open 10am–6pm

NTT InterCommunication Center

Tokyo Metropolitan Government Building

Ethnic Food in Shin-Okubo

The multiethnicity of the new Tokyo can be best experienced in the cosmopolitan, but down-to-earth, Shin-Okubo district. It is home to almost every conceivable Asian nationality, hence its sobriquet, "Little Asia." Apart from Chinese eateries, Korean barbeques, and Burmese restaurants, the area also has several Thai, Indian, and Malaysian curry spots.

5 Tokyo Metropolitan Government Building

Defying time and geology, the Kenzo Tange-designed Tokyo Metropolitan Building (Tocho) stands in the middle of a grove of skyscrapers that have been described as everything from a mini-Manhattan to a row of grave markers. The building's twin 48-story towers have observation rooms. High-speed elevators carry visitors to the sky lounges in less than a minute. The 360-degree views from the top are superlative. Ⓝ Map A4 • 2-8-1 Nishi-Shinjuku, Shinjuku-ku • 5321-1111 • Open 9:30am–11pm Mon, Wed–Sun

6 Shinjuku Gyoen

Part of the estate of the Naito feudal clan, this large garden-park became an imperial retreat in 1906. Now open to the public, it offers Japanese, French, and English gardens, an old glass botanical garden, and a traditional teahouse. Tests have shown that the park is consistently two degrees or more cooler than the surrounding urban area. Ⓝ Map B4 • 11 Naito-cho, Shinjuku-ku • 3350-0151 • Open 9am–4:20pm Tue–Sun • Adm

7 Kabuki-cho

Tokyo's premier *sakariba* (pleasure quarter), Kabuki-cho caters to the city's craving for indulgence. In the words of the American author Donald Richie, this garish, neon-lit district, "concerns itself with the permissive indulgence that the old Edo kept alive on its stage." At night, its dazzling maze of clubs, cabarets, live-music houses, bars, and ethnic restaurants come to life. Ⓝ Map B3 • Kabuki-cho, Shinjuku-ku

8 Hanazono Shrine

With orange pillars and vermillion walls, this shrine was rebuilt several times since it was founded in the 16th century. Its presiding deity is Yamatotaeru-no-Mikoto, a 4th-century warrior. Devotees stop by to petition the gods for luck. Rows

Visitors strolling in the lush garden-park of Shinjuku Gyoen

 A magnate for local events, Hanazono Shrine also hosts a small flea market every Sunday.

A devotee offering prayer, Hanazono Shrine

of red and white paper lanterns illuminate the shrine's entrances at night. ✪ Map B3 • 5-17 Shinjuku, Shinjuku-ku • 3209-5265 • Open dawn–dusk

Golden Gai

A labyrinth of roughly 200 tiny watering holes clusters along Golden Gai's four pedestrian lanes. Dating from just after WWII, these bars are popular with local office workers, and are also patronized by writers, sumo wrestlers, and cross-dressers. Most of the establishments here charge a ¥1000 seating fee for starters. ✪ Map B3 • Shinjuku, Shinjuku-ku

Takashimaya Times Square

A shopping haven, this 15-story department store is stunning in its diversity. Besides the fashion and accessory departments, restaurants, cafés, and well-stocked food basement, there is an IMAX theater, a Sega virtual-reality arcade called Joypolis, and a branch of Tokyu Hands, a novel hardware store. Of special interest to foreigners is a branch of Kinokuniya, a huge bookstore with a floor set aside for books in the English language. ✪ Map B4 • 5-24-2 Sendagaya, Shinjuku-ku • 5361-1111 • Open 10am–8pm

A Day in East Shinjuku

Morning

Leaving the south exit of JR Shinjuku station, walk down to **Shinjuku Gyoen**, a spacious national garden. An entire morning can be spent here, but continue instead to Takashimaya Times Square, a futuristic department store. **Sadeu**, a café on the second floor, serves o-matcha (green tea). Take a short walk along Meiji-dori to the corner of Shinjuku-dori, and **Isetan**, a famous department store and Tokyo institution. The fifth-floor **Isetan Art Gallery** showcases the latest trends in Japan's ceramic, print, and fine-art world. Walk up to Yasukuni-dori, turn left and follow the road to **Tsunahachi** (see p107) on the right. The old wooden restaurant, a postwar survivor, serves tempura lunch sets at moderate prices.

Afternoon

Walk back along Yasukuni-dori until you reach the gates of **Hanazono Shrine**, whose lively grounds are right next to **Golden Gai**, a quadrangle of bars. Its lanes will be empty at this time, a chance to choose the bar you might like to return to. Walk into adjacent Kabuki-cho and take almost any street north toward Okubo-dori, the main street cutting through **Shin-Okubo**. Explore the ethnic food stores and specialist stores in the area. The district has many small temples and fox shrines, as well as Christian churches catering to a large number of Korean worshippers. Have an early dinner at one of the several ethnic restaurants in Shin-Okubo.

Around Town – Shinjuku

Visiting directors, particularly Francis Ford Coppola and Quentin Tarantino, are said to favor La Jetée bar in Golden Gai.

105

Left **Advocates Café** Center **Shinjuku Loft** Right **Oto**

Bars and Music Clubs

1 Clubhouse Tokyo
British and Irish draft beers and a feisty crowd of rugby and soccer fans frequent this very popular sports bar. ⊗ Map B3 • Marunaka Bldg, 3F, 3-7-3 Shinjuku, Shinjuku-ku • 3359-7785

2 Albatross G
The long counter, generous space, and ¥300 seating charge set this place apart from the usual run of cramped Golden Gai bars. ⊗ Map B3 • 2F, 5th Avenue, 1-1 Kabuki-cho, Shinjuku-ku • 3203-3699 • Adm

3 Advocates Café
This gay bar offers happy hour and the Sunday beer binge, where ¥1000 gets you unlimited ale. ⊗ Map B3 • 7th Tenka Bldg, 1F, 2-18-1 Shinjuku, Shinjuku-ku • 3358-3988

4 Shinjuku Loft
This long-established promoter of live rock and pop acts is divided into a main stage and a separate bar area. ⊗ Map B3 • Tatehana Bldg, B2F, 1-12-9 Kabuki-cho, Shinjuku-ku • 5272-0382 • Adm

5 Open
This place is run by people who set up Tokyo's first reggae bar back in the 1990s. ⊗ Map B4 • 2-5-15 Shinjuku, Shinjuku-ku • 3226-8855

6 Bar Plastic Model
A 1980s music soundtrack throbs in the background here at one of Golden Gai's more contemporary theme bars. ⊗ Map B3 • 1-1-10 Kabuki-cho, Shinjuku • 5273-8441

7 Antiknock
Dedicated to rock, this small club showcases new acts, many of them appealing to Tokyo's chic cyber-punks. ⊗ Map B4 • Ray Flat Shinjuku, B1F, 4-3-15 Shinjuku, Shinjuku-ku • 3350-6670

8 Oto
A small-capacity venue with a big sound, Oto has a long interior that attracts those who want to step out to a wide range of dance music. The bar here is decent. Entry fee includes a complimentary drink. ⊗ Map B3 • 2F, 1-17-5 Kabuki-cho, Shinjuku-ku • 5273-8264 • Adm

9 Kinswomyn
Managed by a lesbian activist, this friendly, women-only bar has an English-speaking staff. ⊗ Map B3 • 3F, 2-15-10 Shinjuku, Shinjuku-ku • 3354-8720

10 Shinjuku Pit Inn
Half-price weekend matinees are good value at this club for serious jazz aficionados. There is a sister club in Roppongi. ⊗ Map B3 • B1, 2-12-4 Accord Bldg, Shinjuku • 3354-2024 • Adm

Price Categories

Price ranges are for an average-size dinner for one. Lunchtime menus are often less expensive.

¥	Under ¥2,000
¥¥	¥2,000–¥5,000
¥¥¥	¥5,000–¥10,000
¥¥¥¥	Over ¥10,000

Left **Tenkaippin restaurant**

🔟 Places to Eat

1 Tsunahachi
Whopping portions of deep-fried tempura served in a prewar building offer good value. English menu available. 🕲 *Map B3 • 3-31-8 Shinjuku, Shinjuku-ku • 3352-1012 • ¥*

2 Tokaien
The nine floors of Tokaien serve superb *yakiniku* (Korean-style barbecue). The sixth floor offers an all-you-can-eat menu. 🕲 *Map B3 • 1-6-3 Kabuki-cho, Shinjuku-ku • 3496-1029 • ¥¥*

3 Tenkaippin
Two types of noodle broth are served here: *assari*, thin but flavorsome, and thick *kotteri*. 🕲 *Map B3 • 1-14-3 Kabuki-cho, Shinjuku-ku • ¥¥¥¥*

4 Ban Thai
This popular place is one of Tokyo's first authentic Thai restaurants. 🕲 *Map B3 • Dai-ichi Metro Bldg, 3F, 1-23-14 Kabuki-cho, Shinjuku-ku • 3207-0068 • Closed Sat–Sun • ¥¥*

5 New York Grill
Sunday brunch here is legendary. Excellent meat and seafood dinners. 🕲 *Map B4 • Park Hyatt Hotel, 52F, 3-7-1-2 Nishi-Shinjuku, Shinjuku-ku • 5323-3458 • ¥¥¥¥*

6 Kitchen Shunju
Contemporary Japanese cuisine, tofu dishes, and free-range chicken dishes. 🕲 *Map B3 • Lumine EST, 8F, 3-38-1 Shinjuku, Shinjuku-ku • 5369-0377 • ¥¥*

7 Raj Mahal
The fulsome meat and vegetarian lunch buffet selections makes it a hugely popular choice. 🕲 *Map B4 • 5F, 3-34-11, Shinjuku, Shinjuku-ku • 5379-2525 • ¥¥*

8 Omoide-Yokocho
This atmospheric warren of lanes is full of smoky *yakitori* chicken eateries, noodle stores, and bars. Go now, before inevitable redevelopment claims this place. 🕲 *Map B3 • Nishi-Shinjuku, 1-chome, Shinjuku-ku*

9 Capricciosa
Good-value, no-nonsense pasta dishes are served at this branch of a huge Italian chain. Free coffee appears at the end of meals. 🕲 *B1, 3-27-2 Shinjuku, Shinjuku-ku • 3341-6066 • ¥¥*

10 Imahan
Beefy portions can be expected at this popular *shabu-shabu* and *sukiyaki* eatery. An English menu helps to make the right beef choices. 🕲 *Map B3 • 14F, 5-24-2 Sendagaya, Shibuya-ku • 5361-1871 • ¥¥*

Left **Sengaku-ji Temple** Right **Yokohama waterfront**

Farther Afield

FOR MORE THAN 400 YEARS, *all roads have led to Tokyo, the political, commercial, and cultural axis of Japan. Significant ports, trading posts, temples, mausoleums, and leisure resorts sprang up along these highways. As a result, ideas about architecture, religion, and gardening coursed into the city. A first-rate train service makes it easy to explore beyond the megalopolis, and for sights at the edges of the city, Tokyo's subway system is unmatched. Sumptuous tombs in Nikko, the ancient city of Kamakura, and the Edo-era Kawagoe invoke the past. In contrast, Odaiba Island offers an urbanscape seemingly teleported from the future.*

🔟 Sights

1. Nikko
2. Odaiba Island
3. Kawagoe
4. Yokohama
5. Kamakura
6. Hakone and Mount Fuji
7. Koishikawa Korakuen
8. Sengaku-ji Temple
9. Edo-Tokyo Open-Air Architectural Museum
10. Edo-Tokyo Museum

Engetsukyo Bridge, Koishikawa Korakuen

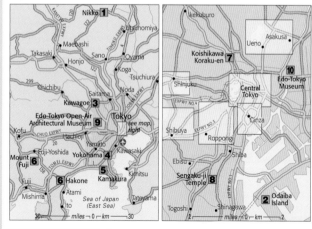

Around Town – Farther Afield

In Nikko, take a bus ride from Toshogu Shrine to the beautiful lake, Chuzenji-ko, and nearby Kegon-no-Taki, an impressive waterfall.

Toshogu Shrine, Nikko

1 Nikko

Nikko's opulent temples, religious art, sacred storehouses, and tombs are more Rococo than Zen. Chosen in 1617 as the burial site of the shogun Ieyasu, Toshogu Shrine is a complex of buildings and mausoleums. It is best accessed by the tree-lined avenue leading to Rinno-ji Temple with its thousand-armed Kannon statue, and Gojuno-to, a five-storied pagoda. Nikko's best-known sight, the Yomei-mon gate to Toshogu Shrine, is lavishly painted and carved. Ieyasu's tomb lies among the cedars a little higher up a forest path. ✪ *Map B1 • Nikko, Tochigi Prefecture • Tobu line from Asakusa • Open 8am–5pm (Dec–Mar: 8am–4pm) • Adm*

2 Odaiba Island

The man-made island of Odaiba presents a shift in time and space with its experimental structures, such as the Fuji TV Building and Tokyo Big Sight. A major hub of culture, shopping, and entertainment, it has fashionable arcades and the cafés and restaurants of Tokyo Decks. Other highlights include a waterfront park, an artificial beach, game centers, and a maritime and high-tech museum *(see pp28–9)*.

3 Kawagoe

Known as "Little Edo," Kawagoe once prospered as a supplier of goods for the capital. Today, its main draw is its high street, Ichiban-gai. Many of its well-preserved warehouses have been converted into stores, galleries, and museums. Yamawa, a ceramic store housed in one of these buildings, is a fine example of the architecture of these fireproof godowns. Toki no Kane, a wooden bell tower down a lane off the main street, has become a symbol of the town. ✪ *Map B2 • Kawagoe, Saitama Prefecture • Tobu Toju line from Ikebukuro*

4 Yokohama

A crucial Meiji-era foreign settlement and port, this waterfront city consists of the huge Minato Mirai complex, with an amusement park, art museum, shopping complex, and Japan's tallest building – the Landmark Plaza. Moored nearby is a fine old clipper, the *Nippon Maru*. The old houses of Yamate (a former foreign residential area), the restaurants and shopping streets of Chinatown, silk and doll museums, old customs buildings, and a lovely Japanese garden, the Sankein, make for a full day. ✪ *Map B2 • Yokohama City • JR Keihin Tohoku line from Tokyo; Minato Mirai subway from Shibuya*

Sculpture at Tokyo Big Sight, Odaiba Island

The warehouses in Kawagoe are made from a mixture of plaster and charcoal powder, giving their surfaces a shiny, black sheen.

109

Glorious bronze statue of the Daibutsu (Great Buddha) looming over visitors in Kamakura

5 Kamakura

The shogun's capital from 1192 to 1333, this seaside town has ancient shrines, gardens, and the Daibutsu Buddha statue, all within an easy train ride of Tokyo. Of its two stations, Kita-Kamakura is close to Engaku-ji Temple and the lush gardens and religious spots of Meigetsu-in. Kamakura Station is close to the local craft and food stores along Wakamiya Oji and Komatsu-dori streets, and to Tsurugaoka Hachiman-gu Temple. ⊗ *Map B2 • JR Yokosuka line from Tokyo, Shimbashi, Shinagawa*

6 Hakone and Mount Fuji

The enjoyable switchback route up the slopes on the Hakone Tozan Railway starts at Hakone-Yumato, a hot spring town. Alight at Miyanoshita, stopping for tea at the Fujiya Hotel *(see p113)*. Farther up, the Hakone Open-Air Museum features sculpture by the likes of Rodin and Henry Moore. Gora is the terminus. Take the funicular and cable car to the shore of Lake Ashi-no-ko, stopping off on the way at Owakudani volcanic springs. Mount Fuji dominates Hakone's landscape. ⊗ *Map A2 • Odakyu express bus from Shinjuku; JR line from Tokyo; Odakyu line from Shinjuku*

7 Koishikawa Korakuen

With an exquisite landscape design dating from 1629, Tokyo's oldest formal garden was created around a central pond. Features replicate scenes found in Japan and China and referred to in literature: a modest hill covered in dwarf bamboo represents Mount Lu; a stream symbolizes a river in Kyoto *(see pp22–3)*.

8 Sengaku-ji Temple

The temple is best known for its association with the "47 Ronin" incident that took place in 1701 *(see p32)*. The retainers of Lord Asano carried their enemy's decapitated head to the temple, placing it on Asano's grave. Well-wishers visit the temple to burn incense at the graves of the faithful *ronin*. ⊗ *Map D2 • 2-11-1 Takanawa, Minato-ku • 3441-5560 • Sengaku-ji, Asakusa subway • Open 7am–5pm (museum: 9am–4pm) • Adm (museum)*

East Meets West

On February 11 1854, Commodore Perry, hoping to open up Japan to foreign trade and diplomacy, sailed "black ships" into Uraga Bay *(see p32)*. The ritual exchange of gifts that ensued – a bronze temple bell and teapot on the Japanese side, a telegraph machine and daguerreotype camera from the visitors – showed how much progress had bypassed Japan.

Mount Fuji's climbing season is limited to July and August. At other times, the 12,388-ft (3,776-m) mountain is covered in snow.

9 Edo-Tokyo Open-Air Architectural Museum

Buildings representative of Tokyo during the Edo, Meiji, and later periods have been collected and reassembled in this fine open-air architectural museum, a branch of the Edo-Tokyo Museum in Ryogoku. The museum's farmhouses, private villas, public buildings, and a bathhouse are set in the middle of Koganei Park. ◎ *Map B2 • 3-7-1 Sakuracho, Koganai Isle • 042-388-3300 • Musashi Koganei, Chuo line • Open Apr–Sep: 9:30am–5:30pm Tue–Sat; Oct–Mar: 9:30am–4:30pm Tue–Sun • Adm • www.tatemonoen.jp*

10 Edo-Tokyo Museum

Housed in an ultramodern building, raised on stilts like an old warehouse, the museum wonderfully evokes the life of ordinary commoners, the merchants, artisans, and craftspeople of the early city, as well as the samurai and aristocracy. It does this in scale display models, costumes, woodblock prints, and other artifacts from the period. The permanent exhibition runs from the building of Edo Castle to the postwar reconstruction and glory days of the 1964 Tokyo Olympics *(see pp14–15)*.

Kabuki costume display, Edo-Tokyo Museum

Two Days in Kamakura

Day 1

Exiting at **Kamakura Station**, take **Komachi-dori**, a street with cafés and specialist stores. Return to the station area and take **Wakamiya-Oji**, a street selling local products. At the end of the road, **Tsurugaoka Hachiman-gu**, Kamakura's premier shrine, is dedicated to the god of war. Back at the entrance, turn left for the **Kamakura National Treasure Hall**.

Stop for excellent noodles at **Nakamura-an**, located along a narrow lane between Wakamiya-Oji and Komachi-dori. Take a bus from the No. 5 stop outside the station to **Sugimoto-dera**, the area's oldest temple. Across the road, **Hokoku-ji Temple** is perfect for tea at the pavilion. A short walk away, **Zuizen-ji** is a Zen temple with a 14th-century garden.

Day 2

Get off at **Kita-Kamakura Station** and stroll down to **Engaku-ji Temple**. Walk over the railroad crossing opposite for **Tokei-ji Temple**. Re-cross the railroad tracks and walk south to **Meigetsu-in Temple**. Return to the road and stroll south toward the wooden gates of **Kencho-ji Temple**. Stop at **Hachi-no-ki Honten** next door for *shojin ryori* (Buddhist vegetarian cuisine). Retrace your steps along the road until you see a hiking path sign. Turn left for the **Daibutsu**, the Great Buddha statue. Follow the road to **Hase-dera Temple**, with a clear view of the bay and town. Take a tram for Kamakura Station at **Hase Station** nearby.

The spacious grounds of Edo-Tokyo Open-Air Architectural Museum are famous for cherry blossoms in early spring.

Left **Metropolitan Art Space building, Ikebukuro** Right **National Sumo Stadium**

Best of the Rest

1 Ikebukuro
The highlights of Ikebukuro, one of Tokyo's main socializing hubs for young people, includes Metropolitan Art Space and Sunshine City complex. 🚫 *Map B2*

2 National Sumo Stadium
Tournaments are held here in alternative months under the the massive Ryogoku Kokugikan stadium. 🚫 *Map B2 • 1-3-28 Yokoami, Sumida-ku • 3623-5111*

3 Shimo-Kitazawa
Fashionable youth fill the narrow jam of streets on weekends for clothing and thrift stores, music clubs, and small, experimental theaters. 🚫 *Map B2*

4 Inokashira Park
A popular cherry blossom-viewing venue in early April. On weekends, musicians, market stalls, and street artists take over its paths. 🚫 *Map B2 • 1-18-31 Gotenyama, Musashino-shi • 0422 47-6900*

5 Ghibli Museum
Attracts admirers of the work of animator Hayao Miyazaki. 🚫 *Map B2 • 1-1-83 Shimo-Renjaku, Mitaka-shi • 00570 05-5777 • Open 10am, 2pm, 4pm Mon, Wed–Sun (tours only) • Adm • www.ghibli-museum.jp*

6 Gotoh Art Museum
A private collection of Buddhist calligraphy, painting, and rare scrolls. 🚫 *Map B2 • 3-9-25 Kaminoge, Setagaya-ku • 3703-0662 • Open 10am–4:30pm Tue–Sun • Adm*

7 Mount Takao
Gentler than climbing Mount Fuji and closer to Tokyo, this quasi-national park has popular hiking trails and an impressive temple, Yakuo-in. 🚫 *Map A2*

8 Tokyo Disney Resort
Disneyland's popular attractions and DisneySea's water-themed attractions should keep the kids happy for the day. 🚫 *Map B2 • 1-1 Maihama, Urayasu-shi, Chiba Prefecture • 045 683-3333 • Adm*

9 Narita Temple
Built in 1940, this lively temple features a drive-in chapel where cars can be blessed, and an important carving of Fudo, the god of fire. 🚫 *Map B2 • 0476-22-2111*

10 Nihon Minka-en
Traditional farmhouses, merchant homes, tools, and domestic utensils have been brought from all over Japan to this open-air folk house museum set in lovely green surroundings. 🚫 *Map B2 • Kawasaki City • 044-922-2181 • Open Mar–Oct: 9:30am–5pm; Nov–Feb: 9:30–4:30pm • Adm*

Ghibli Museum re-creates sections of Hayao Miyazaki's studio, displays film character models, and shows short animations.

Price Categories

Price ranges are for an average-size dinner for one. Lunchtime menus are often less expensive.

¥ Under ¥2,000
¥¥ ¥2,000–¥5,000
¥¥¥ ¥5,000–¥10,000
¥¥¥¥ Over ¥10,000

Left **Shin-Yokohama Ramen Museum** Right **Fujiya Hotel**

Restaurants

1 Shin-Yokohama Ramen Museum

Two floors on the history of Japanese noodles are upstaged by the basement restaurant, which sells Japan's favorite ramen from Hokkaido to Kyushu. ◎ *Map B2 • 2-14-21 Shin-Yokohama, Kohoku-ku • 045 471-0503 • ¥*

2 Dohatsu Honkan

The quality of this long-established restaurant's Hong Kong seafood cuisine is reflected in the long lunchtime lines. The crowd thins a little for dinner. ◎ *Map B2 • 148 Yamashita-cho, Naka-ku • 045 681-7273 • Closed Tue • ¥¥*

3 Mutekkiro

Exquisite French food, with a little French pomp thrown in, is the main draw of this place. The decor and setting, in Yokohama's fashionable Motomachi district, is ideal. ◎ *Map B2 • 2-96 Motomachi, Naka-ku, Yokohama • 045 681-2926 • ¥¥¥*

4 Chaya-kado

Close to Kencho-ji temple, this homely *soba* (buckwheat noodle) restaurant makes a good stop on the temple trail. ◎ *Map B2 • 15-18 Yamanouchi, Kamakura • 0467 23-1673 • ¥*

5 Koko-tei

Tucked away in the Kamakura hills, Koko-tei offers the perfect location for enjoying *kaiseki-ryori*, Japan's multi-course *haute cuisine*. ◎ *Map B2 • 605 Yamanouchi • 0467 46-5467 • ¥¥*

6 Bella Foresta

Located in the grounds of the Hakone Open-Air Museum, Bella Foresta offers a great-value lunch buffet. ◎ *Map A2 • 1121 Ninotaira, Hakone-Machi, Ashigara-Shimogun • 0460 21161 • ¥*

7 Fujiya Hotel

Waitresses in Agatha Christie-era aprons serve delicious Western dishes, such as rainbow trout and sirloin steak. The restaurant's setting has changed little since Fujiya Hotel opened in 1878. ◎ *Map A2 • 359 Miyanoshita • 00560 22211 • ¥¥*

8 Gyoushi-tei

Buddhist vegetarian and *kaiseki-ryori* dishes come with lovely views of moss and pine trees in a park-like setting. A five-minute walk northeast of Rinno-ji temple. ◎ *Map B1 • 1 Yama-uchi • 0288 53-3751 • ¥¥*

9 Hippari Dako

A few minutes short of the entrance to the Toshogu Shrine, this popular *yakitori* (skewered chicken) eatery also serves *yaki-udon* (thick, fried noodles). ◎ *Map B1 • Main road, just before Toshogu complex • 0288 53-2933 • ¥*

10 Ichinoya

Traditional eel dishes, a Kawagoe specialty, are served here on a bed of rice along with miso soup and a dish of pickles. ◎ *Map B2 • 1-18-10 Matsueco, Kawagoe • 00492 22-0354 • ¥¥¥*

Recommend your favorite restaurant on **traveldk.com**

STREETSMART

TOKYO'S TOP 10

Left **Electricity** Center **An aquarium inside a children's park** Right **JAL (Japan Airlines) airplane**

10 Planning Your Trip

1 When to Go
Spring (Apr–May) and fall (Oct–Nov) are the best months for outdoor festivals and cultural events. Pleasantly bearable, winter (Dec–Feb) is a good time to travel, as is mid-Aug (O-Bon Festival). Transportation outside Tokyo can be crowded at these times. Golden Week (Apr 29–May 5) and the New Year (Dec 28–Jan 4) are major vacations, during which there is a stiff rise in flight and accommodation costs.

2 Airlines
JAL (Japan Air Lines), the national airline, offers flights to almost all major destinations in the world. ANA (All Nippon Airways), the second-largest carrier, has a network of international and domestic destinations. Ticket prices are comparable. Most international flights arrive at Narita Airport and domestic flights at Haneda.

3 How Long to Stay
Tokyo's sheer scale and cultural diversity make it a truly infinite city. Time and budget permitting, a stay of up to two weeks is ideal for exploring the city. Visitors planning to also see other parts of Japan should allow at least four or five days for Tokyo.

4 What to Pack
Travel light. The weather can be changeable, so bring varied clothing, or better still, buy some at Tokyo's discount stores. Casual but clean is the general rule for dress in Japan. Shoes that can be slipped on and off are essential. Bring plenty of sun block in the summer. There is no need to pack digital or traditional film, as these are readily available.

5 Passports and Visas
A temporary 90-day visitor visa is issued on arrival to citizens of Western countries. Visa requests can be made at the immigration bureau at least ten days before the original visa expires. The Japan Ministry of Foreign Affairs has a website (www.mofa.go.jp) with a guide to Japanese visas.

6 Language
English signage is excellent, especially in the subways. The largest number of English speakers in Japan are in Tokyo, but don't expect fluency from people on the street. Police officers, taxi drivers, and store attendants are more likely to speak English.

7 Traveling with Children
Tokyo offers countless children-centered activities as well as small parks. Most department stores have a recreation area and sometimes a rooftop play zone.

Drugstores are well stocked for babies. Restaurants usually welcome children, though only large hotels offer babysitting facilities.

8 Time Zone
Tokyo time is nine hours ahead of GMT and 14 hours ahead of US EST. There is no daylight-savings time.

9 Electricity
Japan uses the two-pin type plug common in Asia and North America. The current is 100V AC. Tokyo and the eastern part of Japan are on the 50Hz system. Adaptors are sold at airport camera and electric stores and Tokyo electric stores.

10 Climate
Crisp winter days can be pleasant, often with clear skies. Temperatures occasionally drop below zero, but snow is rare. Spring is generally mild, with some rainfall in late April. June to early July is the rainy season, with high humidity. Those not used to extreme humidity may find the summer months (Jun–early Sep) very hot, with recent temperatures up to 100°F (39°C). Typhoons may hit the city in September, but these are unpredictable. Temperatures drop in fall, with its brilliant foliage and clear skies.

Left **Pleasure boat, Sumida River** Center **Japan Railways staff helping customers** Right **Cycle taxi**

TOP10 Arriving and Getting Around

1 Customs and Immigration

Landing forms and passports are required at the immigration gates. All foreign nationals are fingerprinted before entering the country. Unless you are exceeding the duty-free limit or arriving by ship, no detailed list of your belongings is necessary. There are no restrictions on incoming currency amounts.

2 Airport Facilities

The facilities at Narita International Airport are excellent, with English-speaking staff at information centers. There is also a medical clinic, toilets, and restaurants, as well as several shops and vending machines. Money exchange bureaus and ATMs are plentiful. Facilities for children, such as changing and play areas, are good.

3 Airport Connections

The airports are well run for passengers in transit. Both Narita and Haneda are linked by a first-rate system of trains and buses. Arrive at the airport at least two hours before departure at Narita, and one hour for domestic flights out of Haneda.

4 JR Lines

Japan Railways (JR) dominates Japan's efficient train network. Three lines serve Tokyo. The Yamanote Line (green) runs around central Tokyo and includes all the major stations, which serve as departure points for long-distance travel. The Chuo Line (orange) connects Shinjuku and the western suburbs and Tokyo stations, while the Sobu Line (yellow) serves the eastern suburbs.

5 Tickets and Passes

Valid on all JR lines, JR Suica cards can be bought from "Green Window" counters and vending machines in JR stations. Passnet prepaid travel passes, available in various denominations, cover all Tokyo railway lines and subways, but not JR ones. For travel outside Tokyo, the Japan Railway Pass covers the entire JR network.

6 Subways

There are 14 lines in Tokyo, most run by Tokyo Metro. Four lines (Mita, Oedo, Shinjuku, and Asakusa), called Toei, are run by the metropolitan government. The system is color-coded, but the number of stations and intersecting points can be daunting. Station subway maps in English are available in tourist offices. Look out for the yellow plates outside the ticket wickets showing directions and sights.

7 Buses

Tokyo is served by many bus companies, such as Toei, Keio, and Tokyu, though very few have signs in English. Flat fares (¥200–¥210) are the norm. Prepaid bus passes can be bought at bus stations or from the driver.

8 Taxis

Taxis are expensive, with fares starting at ¥710. Fares are higher on weekends and between 11am and 5pm. A taxi from Narita Airport to the city center will cost at least ¥20,000. Taxi stands can be found near all stations, department stores, and big hotels.

9 Boats

Tokyo has an extensive system of rivers and canals. The Sumida River water bus (*suijo* bus) offers a cruise between Asakusa's Azuma Bridge and the Hama Rikyu Garden. Continue on to Odaiba Marine Park or the Museum of Maritime Science. All boats depart from the Hinode Pier.

10 Bicycling

While it is possible to go sightseeing on foot, Tokyo has some designated bike routes to explore the back alleys of the city. Free bicycles are available every Sunday near Nijubashimae subway for a circuit of the Imperial Place moats. The Meiji Shrine outer gardens have a similar service. Be sure to lock your bicycle to prevent theft.

A special limousine bus operates between Narita and Haneda airports, stopping at hotels and key stations.

Left **English magazines** Center **Bookstore selling books in English** Right **English newspapers**

Sources of Information

1 Tokyo TIC
Tourist Information Centers provide maps, leaflets, itineraries, booklets on Japanese customs, and an accommodation service via the Welcome Inn Reservation Center. Their staff are multilingual. ✪ *Map M4 • 10F, Kotsu-Kaikan Bldg, 2-10-1, Yurakucho, Chiyoda-ku • 3201-3331 • Open 9am–5pm*

2 Japan Travel Phone
The Japan Travel Phone (3201-3331) is a helpful facility for anyone planning trips outside of Tokyo. The English language service operates from 8am to 6pm daily.

3 Websites
The JNTO website is Japan's official travel site. Japan Guide regularly updates its site (www.japan-guide.com) with data on travel and living in Japan. Many major Tokyo sights, especially museums, have their own websites.

4 Newspapers in English
Of Japan's many English-language papers, the long-established *Japan Times* has the best local news and culture coverage, besides international reportage. The *Daily Yomiuri* follows a similar line, with syndicated articles. The *International Herald Tribune* features overseas news.

5 Local Magazines
The quarterly *Tokyo Journal* is the capital's oldest events, people and culture magazine. *JSelect*, a similar magazine, has good Tokyo listings, with features covering Japan. The free weekly *Metropolis* features art, culture, and entertainment listings.

6 English-Language TV and Radio
NHK, the national broadcasting network, operates three satellite and two regular TV channels. Bilingual daily news programs are broadcast at 7 and 9pm. Some films, documentaries, and series are also aired in the bilingual format. Most large hotels provide overseas networks such as BBC and CNN. NHK's AM and FM radio has news and classical music. Some commercial radio stations, such as J-WAVE and Tokyo's InterFM, feature English programs.

7 Entertainment Bookings
Hotels will usually help reserve tickets for entertainment venues. Ticket agency booths located inside department stores, convenience stores, as well as all near train stations also sell last-minute and advance tickets. ✪ *CN Playground: 5802-9999 • Ticket PIA: 5237-9999*

8 Libraries
All of Tokyo's 23 wards have central libraries with a small showing of English books. For ¥500 a day, visitors can use the British Council Library and information center facilities. The Japan Foundation Library has around 30,000 books on Japan, while the National Diet Library has more than 2 million foreign books.

9 Books on Tokyo
Donald Richie's *Tokyo: A View of the City* is a personal account from a resident. In *Tokyo: City of Stories*, Paul Waley explores the city's history through individual areas. Edward Seidensticker's *Low City, High City* and *Tokyo Rising* plot Tokyo's evolution since the Meiji Restoration. *Tokyo: A Cultural History*, by Stephen Mansfield, is a highly acclaimed work.

10 Maps and Local Guides
Periplus and Nelles Maps have laminated maps of Tokyo, while the bilingual *Tokyo City Atlas* provides a detailed mapping. The Japan National Tourist Organization has a free *Tourist Map of Tokyo*. *Tokyo: A Cultural Guide to Japan's Capital City*, by John and Phyllis Martin, presents historical itineraries. *Tokyo Adventures: Glimpses of the City in Bygone Days*, by Tae Moriyama, is a personal guide to an older city.

➤ *English-language newspapers are sold in the larger English-language bookstores, as well as JR and subway station kiosks.*

Left **A typical Japanese restaurant** Right **Senso-ji Temple**

TOP 10 Customs and Etiquette

1 Bathing Customs

Shoes are removed at the entrance to *onsen* (hot springs) and *sento* (public baths). The Japanese thoroughly wash before entering the bath, as it will be used by other people. They wash and rinse sitting at stools in front of low showers and faucets. If there is a plug at the bath, don't pull it; others will be using the same water.

2 Exchanging Business Cards

Always pass a business card to the recipient with both hands, making a bow as the card is proffered. After receiving a card, place it upright on the table. Never write on it, fold it, or tuck it into a pocket.

3 Tipping

Tipping is almost nonexistent in Japan, and may even embarrass some people. The exception is the countryside *ryokan* (Japanese inn), where you should tip the maid who has shown you the room, explained the bedding arrangements, and provided the tea set.

4 Removing Shoes

Wear shoes that are easily removed. Homes, some restaurants, traditional places of accommodation, and the inner areas of some temples have an entrance space where shoes are taken off. If the floor is wooden or tiled, slippers may be provided. Slippers are never worn in rooms with tatami mats. In stores, shoes must be removed before entering the changing rooms.

5 Cell Phones

Etiquette requires people to switch off their cell phones in temples, gardens, and restaurants, though it is often ignored. Subways have signs urging passengers to switch their phones on to "manner mode." On bullet trains, passengers usually go to the space between cars to make their calls.

6 Eating Habits

Chopsticks should never be left stuck in rice. It is good manners to pick up the rice bowl when eating and slurping noodles is the norm. Soup is sipped from the bowl, though the sauce in noodles is eaten with a large spoon. If someone pours you a glass, lift it off the table with both hands. Don't pour your own drink in company.

7 Criticism

Saving face and losing it is still a feature of many Asian countries. In Japan, the shame issuing from public criticism can, in some rare cases, lead to acts of suicide. Avoid severe complaints in public, which can be excruciating for the subject.

8 Gift-Giving

If you are invited to a Japanese home, take flowers, a box of candy, or a souvenir from your own country. An initial show of refusal before accepting a gift is normal. Traditionally, the gift should not be opened in front of the giver. Saying "May I?" is good manners. Gifts should be given and received with both hands.

9 Places of Worship

The Japanese are relaxed in their conduct at temples and shrines. Shinto shrines have a water trough where people purify themselves by washing their hands and rinsing the mouth. Make sure used water is poured on the ground, not back into the basin. Photography is usually permitted in the outer precincts, but be discreet when taking pictures of worshippers. Avoid smoking in the precincts.

10 Personal Questions

The Japanese feel more comfortable with strangers when they know something about their background. Questions about place of birth, age, marital status, and occupation are quite common, so expect some personal inquiries. Women are squeamish about revealing their age. The worst question you can ask a woman is her weight.

In Japan, bits of food should never be passed from one chopstick to another. Don't use chopsticks to take food from a shared plate.

Left **Schoolchildren practising earthquake drill** Center **A local pharmacy** Right **Police station**

⁑10 Security and Health

1 Earthquakes
Earthquake drills take place every September 1, the anniversary of the quake that devastated Tokyo. The usual advice in the event of a quake is to crouch under a heavy table. Make sure all doors are open and gas appliances switched off.

2 Crime
Although theft and random attacks by unhinged individuals have been on the rise, Tokyo remains one of the safest cities in the world. Care should be taken while walking in some crowded areas, such as Kabuki-cho and Roppongi. Hotel staff are scrupulously honest.

3 Health Insurance
Health insurance is recommended, otherwise as a visitor you will be expected to pay the full amount for treatment. Charges for consultations and drugs are high. Be sure to carry proof of health insurance.

4 Pharmacies
Tokyo has a surfeit of well-stocked pharmacies, although the staff may not speak English. The American Pharmacy in the Marunouchi Building (see p68), however, has English-speaking staff.

5 Women Travelers
With a relatively low crime rate, assaults on women travelers are rare. Sexual harassment on trains has been serious enough for some subways to introduce women-only carriages during the rush hours. Some hotels exist exclusively for women. Drunken salarymen can be annoying, but rarely threatening. Ignoring them is the best course.

6 Disabled Travelers
Tokyo is a difficult city for the physically challenged to negotiate, though newer buildings and developments include ramps. Lines of raised dots on the ground guide the visually impaired and traffic lights have audible signals for crossing. Trains have special seats, and many ticket machines have Braille plates.

7 Hospitals
Many hospitals and clinics do not have English-speaking staff. There are some exceptions, such as the Japan Red Cross Medical Center, the Tokyo British Clinic, and the long-established St Luke's International Hospital.

8 Dentists
Dental problems are more self-explanatory than medical ones, so the shortage of English-speaking dentists is not a major problem. Hotel staff can make a recommendation, contact a local clinic, and provide a note in Japanese explaining the problem. The Tokyo Clinic Dental Office has English-speaking staff.

9 Food and Water Safety
Although there have been food-labeling scandals and rice scams recently, the level of quality control and the freshness of food and water in Japan are quite high. Tap water is potable and quite soft.

10 Foreign-Language Helplines
Help and counseling is offered by trained volunteers in a number of languages by the Tokyo English Life Line (TELL). Japan Help Line is a 24-hour nonprofit service.

Directory

Pharmacies
• American Pharmacy: 5220-7716

Hospitals
• Japan Red Cross Medical Center: 3400-1311 • Tokyo British Clinic: 5458-6099 • St Luke's International Hospital: 3541-5151

Dentists
• Tokyo Clinic Dental Office: 3431-4225

Foreign-Language Helplines
• Tokyo English Life Line: 5774-0994
• Japan Help Line: 0570 000 911

For a list of wheelchair-accessible sites in Tokyo, visit the official website of Accessible Japan: **www.wakamoma.org/aj**

Left **Foreign money exchange bureau** Center **Tokyo Big Sight Building** Right **Line outside an ATM**

TOP 10 Banking and Communications

1 Money
Yen banknotes have four denominations: ¥10,000, ¥5,000, ¥2,000, and ¥1,000. The ¥2,000 note is not seen much. Coins can be found in units of ¥500, ¥100, ¥50, ¥10, ¥5, and ¥1. Check exchange rates against your own currency before you travel.

2 Banks
The Bank of Japan (Nippon Ginko) is the country's central banking institution. Along with more local banks, it is not set up to deal with visitors. Main street banks are more geared to visitors' needs. Choose an international bank such as Sumitomo Mitsui, Citibank, or Mizuho Bank. Most banks are open from 9am to 3pm on weekdays.

3 Changing Money
Foreign currencies can be changed and travelers' checks cashed at authorized foreign exchange banks. Some department stores and big hotels change money and travelers' checks. A few foreign exchange bureaus have sprung up in areas visited by tourists.

4 ATMs
Very few standard ATMs accept foreign-issued cards. Citibank has 24-hour international ATMs in Shinjuku and Roppongi. The larger post offices have postal ATMs

linked up to international cash networks. ATMs usually give a slightly better exchange rate than exchanging cash or travelers' checks in department stores and hotels.

5 Credit Cards
Although the Japanese still prefer using cash, large hotels and department stores accept credit cards. American Express, Diners Club, MasterCard, and Visa are the most widely accepted.

6 Telephones, Cards, and Cell Phones
With the exception of train stations and convenience stores, public phones are a rarity. Some phones accept international credit cards. Buy telephone cards from the big telecom companies, such as NTT and KDDI, at kiosks. All major hotels have international dialing. Some foreign cell phones work through operators such as DoCoMo and Softbank Telecom. It is possible to rent or buy a cell phone at provider service desks at Narita and Haneda airports.

7 Post Offices
Yubin-kyoku (post offices) bear the red signs resembling a "T." Mail boxes, too, are red. Post office hours are usually from 9am to 5pm on weekdays. Some main offices open on Saturdays from 9am to 12:30pm.

Express mail services, such as EMS, are reliable. Send priority mail from the Tokyo International Post Office and Tokyo Central Post, each with all-night counters.

8 Internet Cafés
Internet cafés open and close frequently. Yahoo! Japan has cafés at Narita and Haneda airports, and many kissa manga (manga coffee shops) offer cheap access. More reliable is the business service chain, Kinkos, with locations all over Tokyo. There are some clever hackers in Tokyo, so avoid credit card and online banking transactions in net cafés.

9 Television and Radio
The state broadcaster NHK has two local and two satellite TV channels. Tokyo has five other local channels. Satellite broadcaster SkyPerfect! TV has a huge range of channels. InterFM and FEN have music and news.

10 Business Facilities
Large hotels provide space for business-related events. Facilities, such as faxes and Internet access, are usually available. The staff at the Kinkos business service chain speak English. Trade-related exhibitions and business conventions are often held at venues such as Tokyo Big Sight and Tokyo International Forum.

Narita Airport has several foreign exchange bureaus with English-speaking staff. These are open from 7am to 10pm daily.

Left **Budget love hotel** Center **Nezu Jinja Shrine** Right **Live band playing at Yoyogi Park**

Tokyo on a Budget

1 Bargain Accommodations
It is quite possible to find reasonable hotel rooms near train or subway stations in the range of ¥8,000 to ¥10,000. Organizations such as Japan Minshuku Center and Welcome Inn offer a list of cheaper stay options. ✆ *Japan Minshuku Center: 3683 3396* • *Welcome Inn: 3252 1717*

2 Public Transportation
There are a number of good-value travel choices. With a combination of Suica and Passnet, you can take any regular train, subway, or overground line in Tokyo, an economic option for a busy exploration of the city.

3 Cheap Eats
Fierce competition in catering means Tokyo is full of cheap eateries. Lunch sets can be real bargains – chains, such as Yoshinoya, offer lunch and dinner sets for around ¥450. Convenience stores, train stations, and department stores have tasty *bento* boxes. Standalone restaurants and bars are cheap, convivial, and easy to spot.

4 Free Parks and Gardens
Tokyo has over 25,000 parks and gardens, from large open expanses to pocket parks. Free spots, such as Hibiya *(see p74)* and Ueno *(see pp16–17)*

parks, have interesting cultural features including Japanese gardens and temples. The Imperial Palace East Gardens *(see p67)* has historical ruins.

5 Free Days Out
There are many options for cheap days out, with only a subway ticket and convenience store lunch to pay for. Consider walking tours to take in open-air sights, such as the Imperial Palace *(see pp6–7)*; a day people-watching in one of the fashion towns, such as Harajuku; or a half-day in a big street market, such as Ameyoko *(see p50)*.

6 Nights Out
Tokyo prides itself on the beauty of its nighttime illuminations. Besides the colorful neon-covered buildings in the Ginza, Shibuya, and Ikebukuro, many Sumida River bridges *(see pp12–13)* are lit up. Several bars in Roppongi and Shinjuku districts have happy hours before the night gets into full swing.

7 Free Buildings, Museums, and Galleries
For a great city view, the free 45th-floor observation deck at the Tokyo Metropolitan Government Building *(see p104)* is hard to beat. Historic buildings, including the Bank of Japan *(see p68)*, and modern

masterpieces, such as Tokyo International Forum *(see p74)*, are open to the public free of charge. Some first-rate museums, such as the ADMT Advertising Museum *(see p74)*, Tokyo Metropolitan Museum of Photography *(see p35)*, and many Ginza galleries are free.

8 Temples and Shrines
Religious sites rarely charge admission. There are literally thousands of temples and shrines in Tokyo. Among the city's liveliest and architecturally more interesting are Senso-ji Temple *(see pp10–11)* and the Meiji Shrine *(see pp24–5)*.

9 Free Events
Tokyo's rich calendar of cultural events includes festivals, ceremonies, rituals exhibitions, and performances of everything from horseback archery to open-air tea ceremonies and *cosplay* events. See the free weekly *Metropolis* magazine for listings of upcoming events.

10 Discounts
Many places have discounted, and sometimes free, admission to certain categories of people, particularly students and seniors. To qualify, you will need some proof of age, such as a passport or student card.

Left **Traffic congestion** Right **Rush hour lines at a train station**

🔟 Things to Avoid

1 People Jams
Parts of the city can seem monstrously overcrowded. The sidewalks of Shibuya and Shinjuku in particular, and the ticket areas of main stations are often jam-packed. Even pedestrianized streets, such as Takeshita-dori in Harajuku, can be a squeeze. It is best to avoid popular shopping areas on weekends. Intersections, called "scrambles," can become extremely crowded as pedestrians wait for the traffic lights to change.

2 Smoking
Around 40 percent of Japanese people smoke. Tobacco is cheap and vending machines plentiful. Smoking manners are improving, but many people still throw their cigarette butts in the street. Designated non-smoking areas are increasing, but many small restaurants and bars do not have the space or the will to ban smoking. Starbucks has an outside smoking deck.

3 Health Costs
Consultation, treatment, and drug costs at public hospitals and clinics are high. Most hospitals are run as business concerns, so doctors may over-prescribe. Make sure that you have some form of health insurance and carry proof of identity.

4 Red-Light Districts
Organized crime groups are heavily involved in red-light district businesses. Although they are generally fairly safe to walk through at night, it is inadvisable for women to stroll through the back lanes of these areas unaccompanied.

5 Visiting Sights on National Holidays
Famous sights can get extremely crowded on national holidays, especially when the weather is pleasant. If you can only go sight-seeing on these days, try leaving before 10am.

6 Driving in Tokyo
As the roads in Tokyo are narrow and crowded, driving may not be a good idea. While bumper-to-bumper jams are common, the sheer complexity of the city can have disastrous results, especially if you miss a turn. On the plus side, directions are clear and signage easy to understand, even though there are very few signs in English. Driving manners are, by and large, reasonable. The Japanese drive on the left.

7 Eating and Drinking on Trains
Time-pressed passengers may sometimes snack on trains, but in general, eating and drinking in subways is frowned upon. For longer journeys outside the city, boxed lunches, called *ekiben*, are popular. Drinking, including beer, is fine.

8 Subway Confusion
English signage in subways is usually very good, but the mass of passengers and the unfamiliar surroundings can be dizzying. Long underground corridors and the large number of exits add to the confusion. Station maps and exit listings are useful. Some subway workers are trained to give directions in English.

9 Rush Hours
The subway crush runs approximately from 7 to 9am and from 5 to 7:30pm. Some lines, including the Ginza and Tozai, are always busy. Try to edge close to the door before you reach your station, and avoid the last, jam-packed train of the day.

10 Train Drunks
Drunks can occasionally be a problem. People rarely reprimand drinkers. Some boozers on late-night subways and over-ground trains can become loud or over-familiar. They are also quite likely to collapse or vomit without warning. If you sense trouble, move to the next car.

Left **An array of fans** Center **Mitsukoshi department store** Right **Takeshita-dori fashion street**

🔟 Shopping Tips

1 What to Buy
In Tokyo, consumer culture finds outlets everywhere, with fashion and food being the brand areas the city excels at. Craft stores sell ceramics, textiles, lacquer, and paper goods. Galleries and specialist stores offer traditional as well as modern artworks.

2 Shopping Hours
Individual shops and department stores are usually open from 10am to 8pm. Some stores stay open until 10pm. Department stores are open daily, smaller stores may be closed on Monday or Wednesday. Most stores remain open on national holidays and Sundays. Christmas is not a holiday, but many shops close on New Year's Day.

3 Credit Cards
Japan has been slow to take up the use of credit cards, and it is useful to carry some cash. All the department stores, large clothing chains, and many souvenir stores accept cards (see p121).

4 Tax Refunds
Most department stores and electrical goods stores in places such as Akihabara offer tax exemptions for purchases over ¥10,000. After paying, take the goods, your receipts, and passport to the tax-refund counter for reimbursement.

5 Fashion Districts
There are no hard and fast rules about where to shop, but Tokyo's fashion districts tend to be quite generational. Ginza and Aoyama attract a middle-aged, well-heeled crowd, though some stores have been making a bid for the youth market. Harajuku appeals to mid-teens, Shibuya to high-teens to those in their early 20s, Shimokitazawa to the college crowd, and Naka-Meguro and Daikanyama to 20- and 30-somethings.

6 Electronics, Gadgets, and Gizmos
Akihabara, or "Electric Town," as it is called, is the world's largest electronic center, stocking everything from portable music units to robot pets and toys, all at very competitive prices. Big stores can be found close to other major Yamanote line stations.

7 Department Stores
Tokyo's department stores are a great shopping experience. Typically, the first floors sell women's clothing and accessories, with menswear on the floor above. Food basements are known for their delicacies. Stores are lifestyle complexes, places where people stop for coffee or lunch, to relax in a rooftop beer garden, to take in an exhibition, or join a culture class.

8 Bookstores
Tokyo has several excellent bookstores stocking English titles. The biggest are Maruzen in Nihonbashi, the Oazu complex in Marunouchi, Kinokuniya's two stores in Shinjuku (see p50), and the Yaesu Book Center near Tokyo station. Tower Records' bookstore (see p51) is one of the best. Good Day Books and Blue Parrot sell used books. ✆ Good Day Books: Map C2; 3F Asahi Building, 1-11-2 Ebisu, Shibuya-ku • Blue Parrot: Map C1; Takadanobaba, JR Station

9 Music
Tokyo has countless new and used record stores. Tower Records' Shibuya store has six floors of music. Nearby, HMV is massive. If there is something you missed the first time round, Shibuya and Shinjuku's used CD and vinyl stores, which includes Recofan and Disk Union, may be the place to find it.

10 Souvenirs, Arts, and Crafts
The well-stocked Oriental Bazaar (see p53) is an exellent gift store. The Japan Traditional Craft Center (see p53) sells the work of craftsmen from all over Japan. Specialist stores include Hara Shobo (see p52) for woodblock prints, Isetatsu (see p52) for paper, and Fuji Torii (see p50) for antiques.

Tokyo's department stores (depatos) also sell tickets for concerts and exhibitions.

Left **Vegetarian plastic food model** Center **Ordering and paying** Right **Basement food at a store**

TOP 10 Eating and Accommodation Tips

1 Ordering and Paying
In most places, the waiter will automatically come for your order. Many restaurants have photo menus and plastic food displays in the window. Waiters come to your table with the bill, which you then take to the cash register to pay. You can place your money on a small dish and the change will be put back on the dish with the receipt.

2 Tipping and Service
There is no custom to tip in Japan, with the exception of expensive Western-style restaurants. At a high-end *ryokan* (traditional Japanese inn) it is normal to leave a ¥1,000 tip for the maid who settles you into your room. Service standards at restaurants, hotels, and inns are some of the highest in the world.

3 Vegetarian Deals
Tokyo can be a difficult city for vegetarians to get by in, but things are improving. The district of Aoyama has a number of vegetarian restaurants, including Natural Harmony Angolo and the wholefood Mominoki House.

4 Ethnic Food
It is possible to find Thai and Indian restaurants in almost any district of Tokyo. One of the city's best places to sample ethnic food is Shin-Okubo (see p104), which serves Burmese, Indonesian, Korean, Malaysian, as well as Nepalese dishes.

5 Basement Food
Department stores offer a wide range of pastries, Japanese sweets, cured and dried seafood, and wines. In addition to these, there are counters where one can expect to find dishes such as sushi and *tonkatsu* (deep-fried pork cutlets). Isetan, Tobu, Mitsukoshi, and Takashimaya stores are well known for the quality and selection of food items in their basements.

6 Making Reservations
Make reservations at top-end restaurants. Those that require advance booking on the phone usually have English-speaking staff. If not, your hotel may be able to help. You don't generally need to reserve at medium-range eateries unless you are in a group.

7 Tax and Service Charges
All hotels charge a 5 percent tax, with an extra 3 percent if the bill comes to over ¥15,000 a night. High-end hotels include a service charge of 10 to 15 percent for rooms. Only very classy restaurants impose a service charge.

8 Minshuku
Minshuku are friendly, family-run places where it is easy to meet other travelers. Similar to B&Bs, average room charges range from ¥6,000 to ¥7,000. There are only a small number of *minshuku* in Tokyo, but plenty of budget places that are known as *ryokan* (see p132), though they are almost the same. Payment is accepted in cash only.

9 Peak Seasons
Narita and Haneda airports get extremely crowded during the three big vacations at New Year (Dec 25–Jan 4), Golden Week (Apr 29–May 5), and O-Bon (mid-Aug). It is always best to book accommodation well in advance. Cheaper rooms especially can get booked out in February when thousands of students arrive in Tokyo for the university entrance exams.

10 Ryokan Rules
When entering a *ryokan*, shoes must be removed and exchanged for house slippers laid outside. Slippers should be taken off before stepping on the tatami mats in your room. If the bath is communal, you should put on the *yukata* (cotton robe) provided. While the smaller *ryokan* has only one bath, a larger one has segregated bathing.

The tokonoma (alcove) in a corner of the room at a ryokan is to be respected. Do not leave suitcases, ashtrays, or drinks on it.

Left **Exterior, Hilton Hotel** Center **Hotel Seiyo Ginza** Right **Mandarin Oriental Tokyo**

TOP 10 Luxury Hotels

1 ANA Intercontinental Tokyo

Part of the Ark Hills complex, the hotel has a well-sized lobby and spacious rooms. Upper-floor rooms and a rooftop pool offer views of Tokyo and Mt. Fuji. ◈ *Map J5 • 1-12-23 Akasaka, Minato-ku • 3505-1111 • www.anaintercontinental-tokyo.jp/e/ • ¥¥¥¥¥*

2 Grand Hyatt Tokyo

Luxurious rooms come with modern facilities. The blend of modern interior design and natural elements creates a tasteful ambience. Restaurants, a patisserie, and spa. ◈ *Map C6 • 6-10-3 Roppongi, Minato-ku • 4333-1234 • www.tokyo.grand.hyatt.com • ¥¥¥¥¥*

3 The Prince Park Tower Tokyo

Opened in 2005, this 33-floor luxury hotel offers spacious rooms with Internet access, jet baths, and balconies with views of Shiba Park and Mt. Fuji. Set in landscaped gardens. ◈ *Map E6 • 4-8-1 Shibakoen, Minato-ku • 5400-1111 • www.princehotels.co.jp • ¥¥¥¥*

4 Le Meridien Grand Pacific Tokyo

A sumptuous hotel with excellent service and first-rate facilities. Superb views of the bay and skyscrapers along the waterfront from rooms on the middle to upper floors, and from the 30th-floor Sky Lounge. ◈ *Map D2 • 2-6-1 Daiba, Minato-ku • 5500-6711 • www.htl-pacific.co.jp • ¥¥¥¥*

5 Yokohama Royal Park Hotel

This hotel is ideal for those looking for great views. Rooms are located on the 52nd to 67th floors of the Landmark Tower, Japan's tallest building, offering splendid views of the waterfront and Mt. Fuji. ◈ *Map B2 • 2-2-1 Minato-ku, Nishi-ku, Yokohama • 045-221-1111 • www.yrph.com • ¥¥¥¥*

6 Hilton Hotel

Recent renovation upgraded Asia's biggest Hilton. Newly decorated rooms have cable TV and modems. Has an indoor heated swimming pool, gym, restaurants, bars, shops, and night views of the skyscraper district. ◈ *Map A3 • 6-6-2 Nishi-Shinjuku, Shinjuku-ku • 3344-5111 • www.hilton.com • ¥¥¥¥¥*

7 Claska

It is worth the slightly inconvenient location to experience the epitome of luxury at this ultra-modern, two-floor hotel. Each room has a different design, but all are spacious and original in concept. Includes a gallery, bookstore, and restaurant-bar. ◈ *Map C2 • 1-13-18 Chuo-cho, Meguro-ku • 3719-8121 • www.www.claska.com • ¥¥¥¥*

8 Mandarin Oriental Tokyo

Japanese artisan materials, such as paper lanterns, hanging textiles, and traditional furnishings, embellish the rooms and lobby of this distinguished hotel. Views of Mt. Fuji and night scenes of the famous business district add charm. ◈ *Map N2 • 2-1-1 Nihonbashi-Marumachi, Chuo-ku • 3270-8800 • www.mandarinoriental.com/tokyo • ¥¥¥¥¥*

9 Hotel Seiyo Ginza

A private club mood prevails at this elegant hotel. Each room comes with its own valet. Ideally placed to explore the Ginza and Marunouchi shopping and entertainment districts. The on-site Italian and Japanese *kaiseki ryori* restaurant is exceptional. ◈ *Map N4 • 1-11-2 Ginza, Chuo-ku • 3535-1111 • www.seiyo-ginza.com • ¥¥¥¥¥*

10 Imperial Hotel

With a history dating from the 1890s, the Imperial Hotel enjoys unimpeachable credentials. Rooms on the new floor are slightly larger and come with a flat-screen TV. Conveniently located across Hibiya Park (see p74), it is a short stroll away from the Ginza district. ◈ *Map L4 • 1-1-1 Uchisaiwaicho, Chiyoda-ku • 3504-1111 • www.imperialhotel.co.jp • ¥¥¥¥¥*

Streetsmart

Unless otherwise stated, all hotels accept credit cards and have en-suite bathrooms and air conditioning.

Left **Hotel Villa Fontaine Shiodome** Right **Shinjuku Washington Hotel**

🔟 Mid-Range Hotels

1 Hotel Kokusai Kanko

Located close to the north end of Tokyo Station, this no-frills, eight-story hotel offers decent single and family rooms. Facilities include a restaurant, lunch corner, coffee shop, bar, lounge. English-speaking staff. ◈ *Map M3 • 1-8-3 Marunouchi, Chiyoda-ku • 3215-3281 • ¥¥¥*

2 Granbell Hotel

This cheerful hotel with a calm atmosphere is only a short walk from Shibuya Station. Double and single rooms have light furnishings and colors. There is one super, but more expensive, maisonette-style terrace suite. ◈ *Map R6 • 15-17 Sakuragaoka-cho, Shibuya-ku • 5457-2681 • www.granbellhotel.jpl • ¥¥¥*

3 Tokyo Green Hotel

Reasonably-priced, cozy rooms are provided at this Japanese contemporary hotel. Facilities include an attractive restaurant and a bar. Close to Ochanomizu, the Jimbocho book district, and the electronics hub of Akihabara. ◈ *Map F2 • 2-6 Kanda-Awajicho, Chiyoda-ku • 3255-4161 • www.greenhotel.co.jp • ¥¥*

4 Roppongi Prince Hotel

Since it opened in 1984, this hotel has not seen much change, still retaining its original charm. A relaxed place to stay, with well-sized rooms, friendly staff, and a heated outdoor pool. Just a few minutes' walk from Roppongi. ◈ *Map J5 • 3-2-7 Roppongi, Minato-ku • 3587-1111 • ¥¥¥*

5 Creston Hotel

This stylish hotel can be found down a quiet backstreet equidistant from Bunkamura *(see p96)* and the NHK complex. A great location for exploring Shibuya's nightlife and restaurant scene. English-speaking staff. ◈ *Map Q4 • 10-8, Kamiyama-Cho, Shibuya-ku • 3481-5800 • www.crestonhotel.co.jp • ¥¥¥*

6 Hotel Mets Shibuya

With an exceptional location right next to Shibuya Station, the Mets Shibuya has attractive rooms and some great-value deluxe singles. (But try to book one away from the railway tracks.) The room price includes a buffet breakfast. ◈ *Map S5 • 3-29-17 Shibuya, Shibuya-ku • 3409-0011 • www.hotelmets.jp/shibuya • ¥¥¥*

7 Shinjuku Washington Hotel

The rooms at this business hotel are basic, but the amenities and service are good. The views from the upper floors of neon-lit Shinjuku are stunning. There is a women-only floor. ◈ *Map A4 • 3-2-9 Nishi-Shinjuku, Shinjuku-ku • 3343-3111 • www.wh-rsv.com/english/shinjuku • ¥¥¥*

8 Ginza Nikko Hotel

Attracting business and leisure travelers, this hotel offers cheerful rooms with large bathtubs, quite a luxury for Tokyo. Well-placed for Ginza shopping. Good value, given the posh neighborhood. ◈ *Map M5 • 8-4-21 Ginza, Chuo-ku • 3571-4911 • www.ginza-nikko-hotel.com • ¥¥¥*

9 Hotel Kazusaya

In the center of Tokyo's business district, this hotel provides decent-sized, well-furnished Japanese- and Western-style rooms. Facilities include a good restaurant and Internet access. ◈ *Map P1 • 4-7-15 Nihonbashi-Honcho, Chuo-ku • 3241-1045 • www.h-kazusaya.co.jp • ¥¥*

10 Hotel Villa Fontaine Shiodome

Part of a hotel chain that keeps its prices low and standards high, this 2004 flagship is located in the dazzling Shiodome complex *(see p74)*. Small but creatively designed rooms come with free broadband Internet access. There are some women-only floors. ◈ *Map M6 • 1-9-2 Higashi-Shimbashi, Minato-ku • 3569-2220 • www.hvf.jp/shiodome • ¥¥¥*

Left **Shinjuku Urban Hotel** Center **Capsule Hotel Riverside** Right **Sakura Hotel**

🔟 Budget Hotels

1 Capsule Hotel Riverside

If you would like to try one capsule hotel *(see p45)*, the Riverside is a good option. A fun experience for a night, it offers sauna and bath facilities. Each unit has a mini-TV hinged to the wall. Both men and women are accepted. ◎ *Map R2 • 2-20-4 Kaminarimon, Taito-ku • 3844-5117 • www.asakusa-capsule.jp/english • ¥*

2 Hotel New Koyo

Spotlessly clean, the tiny Japanese- and Western-style rooms at this hotel in the day-laborer district of Sanya are popular with back-packers. English-speaking staff. ◎ *Map H1 • 2-26-13 Nihonzutsumi, Taito-ku • 3878-0343 • www. newkoyo.com • ¥*

3 Shibuya City Hotel

Surprisingly good value for clean, spacious rooms, this small hotel is located close to Bunkamura and the music clubs and restaurant life of Shibuya. The friendly staff can get by in English. ◎ *Map A6 • 1-1 Maruyama-cho, Shibuya-ku • 5489-1010 • www. shibuya-city-hotel.com • ¥¥*

4 P & P Plaza

A famous love hotel in Shibuya's Dogenzaka Hill area. Room themes range from Moroccan and British Royal to Neo-Japanesque and tropical

resort. One of the more expensive ninth-floor suites has a swimming pool. Couples only. ◎ *Map R6 • 1-17-9 Dogenzaka, Shibuya-ku • 3780-5211 • www.p-plaza.com • ¥*

5 YMCA Asia Youth Center

More like a hotel than a hostel, this establishment has comfortable, though rather small, Western-style rooms and en-suite bathrooms. Also has a restaurant and Internet terminals for guests. ◎ *Map E3 • 2-5-5 Sarugakucho, Chiyoda-ku • 3233-0611 • www. ymcajapan.org/ayc • ¥*

6 Sakura Hotel

A popular choice with moderate- and budget-range travelers, this hotel offers accommodation options including shared dorms and miniscule, but cozy, private rooms, all non-smoking. The friendly English-speaking staff and a good location are bonuses. ◎ *Map L1 • 2-21-4 Kanda-Jimbocho, Chiyoda-ku • 3261-3939 • www.sakura-hotel.co.jp • ¥*

7 Asia Center of Japan

Well served by subways and in the heart of fashionable Aoyama, the Asia Center has all the facilities of a business hotel at affordable rates. Rooms in the old annex are basic but spacious; those in the newer building are Western-style.

Offers a hearty breakfast buffet. ◎ *Map C5 • 8-10-32 Akasaka, Minato-ku • 3402-6111 • www. asiacenter.or.jp • ¥*

8 Hotel Sunlite Shinjuku

This well-run, middle- to cheap-range business hotel has simple rooms with good facilities. Its location on the east side of Shinjuku Station, close to a major shopping area and the entertainment district of Kabuki-cho, is a bonus. ◎ *Map B3 • 5-15-8 Shinjuku, Shinjuku-ku • 3356-00391 • www. sunlite.co.jp/top-e.htm • ¥¥*

9 Shinjuku Urban Hotel

Its location right in the center of the Kabuki-cho entertainment area makes up for this hotel's lack of charm. Rooms are clean and decently sized. The staff know very little English, but are friendly and willing. ◎ *Map B3 • 2-8-12 Kabuki-cho, Shinjuku-ku • 3209-1231 • ¥¥*

10 Tokyo International Youth Hostel

A modern hostel on the 18th and 19th floors of Central Plaza. Except for a Japanese-style family room, accommodation is in shared dorms. A souvenir store, dining hall, Internet access, and a TV in the lobby. ◎ *Map D3 • 18F, 21-1 Kagurakashi, Shinjuku-ku • 3235-1107 • www.tokyo-ih.jp • ¥*

 Unless otherwise stated, all hotels accept credit cards and have en-suite bathrooms and air conditioning.

Price Categories

For a standard, double room per night, including taxes and service charges.

¥	Under ¥8,000
¥¥	¥8,000–¥15,000
¥¥¥	¥15,000–¥25,000
¥¥¥¥	¥25,000–¥35,000
¥¥¥¥¥	Over ¥35,000

Shibuya Tobu Hotel

Streetsmart

🔟 Business Hotels

1 Mitsui Urban Hotel Ginza

This business hotel has two floors of restaurants, a bar, room service till midnight, broadband Internet access, and slightly above average-sized rooms. Convenient location for shopping and sightseeing in the Ginza area. 🖙 Map M5 • 8-6-15 Ginza, Chuo-ku • 3527-4131 • www.granvista.co.jp • ¥¥¥

2 Hotel Arca Torre Roppongi

The street life can be a tad noisy at times, but the rooms at this well-appointed hotel are comfortable. Located right next to the Roppongi Crossing and a short hop to Roppongi Hills. 🖙 Map D6 • 6-1-23 Roppongi, Minato-ku • 3404-5111 • www.arktower.co.jp • ¥¥¥

3 Tokyo Bay Ariake Washington Hotel

With 20 floors, this reasonably large business hotel is preferred by travelers attending exhibitions at nearby Tokyo Big Sight (see p44). Excellent amenities with over 750 rooms and Japanese and Western restaurants. 🖙 Map D2 • 3-1 Ariake, Koto-ku • 5564-0111 • www.wh.rsv.com • ¥¥¥

4 Shibuya Tobu Hotel

Unusually stylish-looking lobby, elegant furnishings, and rooms featuring lots of marble and wood trim. The restaurants serve various cuisines. The semi-double beds in the slightly more expensive singles are worth going for. 🖙 Map R5 • 3-1 Udagawa-cho, Shibuya-ku • 3476-0111 • www.tobuhotel.co.jp/shibuya • ¥¥¥

5 Hotel Excellent

With basic facilities and little character, this place has an excellent location, just one minute from Ebisu station. Pleasant, well-maintained rooms and low rates make it a decent choice. No on-site restaurant, but there are many good dining options close by. 🖙 Map C2 • 1-9-5 Ebisu-Nishi, Minato-ku • 5458-0087 • ¥¥

6 Akasaka Yoko Hotel

A good option if you wish to be close to the Roppongi nightspots, but far enough away to get a decent sleep. The hotel's design is rather modest, but the facilities are good and the friendly staff always on hand. 🖙 Map D5 • 6-14-12 Akasaka, Minato-ku • 3586-4050 • www.yokohotel.co.jp/english/ • ¥¥

7 Yaesu Terminal Hotel

Modern, understated decor and furnishings make up for the rather smallish rooms at this hotel. Its location, a short walk from Tokyo Station and the Ginza and Yurakucho districts, is another plus. 🖙 Map N3 • 2-9-1 Yaesu, Chuo-ku • 3273-2111 • www.yaesufujiya.com/english • ¥¥¥

8 Kayabacho Pearl Hotel

Located beside a canal in the business district of Kayabacho, this slightly high-end business hotel has spacious, well decorated and furnished rooms, a business center, a good all-purpose restaurant, and English-speaking staff. 🖙 Map P3 • 1-2-5 Shinkawa, Chuo-ku • 3553-8080 • www.pearlhotel.co.jp/kayabacho • ¥¥¥

9 Hotel Sunroute Asakusa

Ideal for visitors who want to stay in simple, Western-style rooms in the traditional district of Asakusa. Well-managed and good value. The family restaurant, Jonathan's, is on the second floor. 🖙 Map Q2 • 1-8-5 Kaminarimon, Taito-ku • 3847-1511 • ¥¥¥

10 Ueno First City Hotel

Peaceful, comfortable, and efficiently run, this hotel is located closer to Yushima than Ueno. All the Western- and Japanese-style rooms come with en-suite bathrooms. 🖙 Map F2 • 1-14-8 Ueno, Taito-ku • 3831-8215 • www.uenocity-hotel.com • ¥¥

Left **Hotel Nikko Tokyo** Right **Cerulean Tower Tokyu Hotel**

⑩ Rooms with a View

① Hotel Parkside
This good-value hotel offers Japanese- and Western-style rooms. Rooms on the middle to upper floors have the finest views of the park and lotus pond, which is at its best in summer. ⑤ *Map F2 • 2-11-18 Ueno, Taito-ku • 3836-5711 • www.parkside.co.jp • ¥¥¥*

② Conrad Hotel
The city views and aerial perspectives on to the green and watered Hama Rikyu Garden *(see p75)* below, from this 37-story upmarket hotel, are unparalleled. Aromatic therapies, cedar wood spas, and superb cuisine make a stay here memorable. ⑤ *Map L6 • 1-9-1 Higashi-Shimbashi, Minato-ku • 6388-80000 • www.conradtokyo.co.jp • ¥¥¥¥¥*

③ Palace Hotel
With one of the best hotel locations in Tokyo, this serenely quiet, old-fashioned establishment has spacious rooms offering superb views of the Imperial Palace *(see pp8–9)*. Excellent on-site restaurant. ⑤ *Map M2 • 1-1-1 Marunouchi, Chiyoda-ku • 3211-5211 • www.palacehotel.co.jp • ¥¥¥¥¥*

④ Cerulean Tower Tokyu Hotel
Shibuya's only high-end luxury hotel boasts huge rooms, stylish interiors, *kaiseki* restaurants, bars, a jazz club, and Noh Theater *(see p58)*. Rooms with breathtaking views are located between the 13th and 37th floors. ⑤ *Map R6 • 26-1 Sakuragaoka-cho, Shibuya-ku • 3476-3000 • www.ceruleantower-hotel.com/en • ¥¥¥¥*

⑤ Park Hyatt Tokyo
Remember the grandstand views Scarlett Johansson looked out on from her room at this hotel in the movie *Lost in Translation*? They are even better at night, when Shinjuku's neon is switched on. The reception desk is on the 41st floor. ⑤ *Map A4 • 3-7-1-2 Nishi-Shinjuku, Shinjuku-ku • 5322-1234 • http://tokyo.park.hyatt.com • ¥¥¥¥¥*

⑥ Shinjuku Prince Hotel
Next to JR Shinjuku Station, this cozy hotel offers stunning views of the Kabuki-cho entertainment, club, and bar area from guest rooms and its 25th-floor restaurant. Good facilities and reasonably sized rooms. ⑤ *Map B3 • 1-30-1 Kabuki-cho, Shinjuku-ku • 3205-1111 • www.princehotels.co.jp • ¥¥¥*

⑦ Asakusa View Hotel
As the name suggests, the views of neighboring rooftops and nearby Senso-ji Temple *(see pp10–11)* from the comfortable Japanese-style rooms are of an older Tokyo. The 28th-floor bar has the best views of Sumida River and its bridges *(see pp12–13)*. ⑤ *Map Q1 • 3-17-1 Nishi-Asakusa, Taito-ku • 3847-1111 • www.viewhotels.co.jp/asakusa/english • ¥¥¥*

⑧ Inter Continental Tokyo Bay
The views from the stylish rooms here are truly panoramic. Windows face onto the river, Tokyo wharves, Tokyo Bay, and neon-illuminated Rainbow Bridge, as it crosses to Odaiba Island *(see pp28–9)*. ⑤ *Map C2 • 1-16-2 Kaigan, Minato-ku • 5404-2222 • www.intercontinental.com • ¥¥¥¥¥*

⑨ Hotel Nikko Tokyo
This well-appointed hotel is located next to the Tokyo Decks' leisure, café, and restaurant complex. The windows of its luxurious rooms offer stunning vistas of the bay, island, and waterfront. ⑤ *Map D2 • 1-9-1 Daiba, Minato-ku • 5500-5511 • www.hnt.co.jp • ¥¥¥¥¥*

⑩ The Westin Tokyo
Modeled along the lines of grand European hotels, the Westin stands just beyond the Ebisu Garden Place complex. Views from the middle and upper rooms toward the bay and inward over the glittering city are stunning. ⑤ *Map C2 • 1-4-1 Mita, Meguro, Minato-ku • 5423-7000 • www.westin-tokyo.co.jp • ¥¥¥¥¥*

Unless otherwise stated, all hotels accept credit cards and have en-suite bathrooms and air conditioning.

Yaesu Fujiya Hotel

TOP 10 Hotels Handy for Sightseeing

1 Peninsula Hotel Tokyo

Completed in 2008, this highly reputed 24-story hotel is close to the Imperial Palace East Gardens (see p67), Hibiya Park (see p74), and Tokyo International Forum (see p74). The Ginza shopping center is a short stroll away. ⊗ Map M4 • 1-8-1 Yurakucho, Chiyoda-ku • 6270-2888 • www. peninsula.com/Tokyo • ¥¥¥

2 Hotel Ibis

This Ibis flagship is favored by ravers whose sightseeing priorities are for the Roppongi clubs and bars. Although newer hotels are giving it stiff competition, it still offers good value. Friendly staff and the excellent Sabatini Italian restaurant. ⊗ Map C6 • 7-14-4 Roppongi, Minato-ku • 3403-4411 • www.ibis-hotel.com • ¥¥¥

3 Excel Hotel Tokyu

Located in the Mark City shopping and restaurant complex, right next to the station, this hotel is the closest one can get to Shibuya's lively day and night activities. Spacious rooms have good views. Two women-only floors. ⊗ Map R5 • 1-12-2 Dogenzaka, Shibuya-ku • 5457-0109 • www. tokyuhotels.co.jp • ¥¥¥

4 Keio Plaza Hotel

One of the best bases for visiting the sights of Shinjuku. Given its location among the skyscrapers of West Shinjuku and first-rate amenities, including heated pools, stores, and restaurants, room rates are reasonable. ⊗ Map A4 • 2-2-1 Nishi-Shinjuku, Shinjuku-ku • 3344-0111 • www.keioplaza. co.jp • ¥¥¥

5 Century Hyatt Tokyo

The hotel's exterior may not be particularly striking, but once inside, the roomy lobby, spacious rooms, and superlative service guarantee comfort and exclusivity. Close to all the Shinjuku sites, including the Tokyo Metropolitan Building (see p104). ⊗ Map A3 • 2-7-2 Nishi-Shinjuku, Shinjuku-ku • 3348-1234 • www.tokyo.century.hyatt. com • ¥¥¥

6 Star Hotel Tokyo

Although there are no luxurious surroundings, this modest hotel has clean rooms, a helpful staff, and a location only minutes away from the sights of Shinjuku. An outstanding deal for travelers on a budget. ⊗ Map A3 • 7-10-5 Nishi-Shinjuku, Shinjuku-ku • 3361-1111 • www.starhotel. co.jp/city/tokyo • ¥¥

7 Yaesu Fujiya Hotel

Decent-sized rooms, most of them recently renovated, and good service make this business hotel an excellent sightseeing option. Conveniently located for Tokyo Station and within a short stroll to Yurakucho. ⊗ Map N4 • 2-9-1 Yaesu, Chuo-ku • 3273-2111 • www.yaesufujiya.com • ¥¥¥

8 Hotel Alcyone

Close to the Kabuki-za Theater (see p73), stores, and nightlife of the Ginza this hospitable hotel, converted from a former ryokan, has both Japanese and Western rooms. ⊗ Map N5 • 4-14-3 Ginza, Chuo-ku • Map XX • 3541-3621 • www.hotel-alcyone.co.jp • ¥¥

9 Four Seasons Hotel Tokyo Marunouchi

Close to Tokyo Station and the Imperial Palace (see pp8–9), this luxurious hotel offers large rooms with wide-screen plasma TV, DVD players, and great views. Service from the multilingual staff is impeccable. ⊗ Map M3 • Pacific Century Plaza, 1-11-1 Marunouchi, Chiyoda-ku • 5222-7222 • www.fourseasons.com/marunouchi • ¥¥¥¥¥

10 Ueno Tsukuba Hotel

An affordable option for sightseeing in Ueno, this business hotel provides small-sized rooms. Opt for the slightly larger Japanese rooms, though you will have to share the first-floor communal bath if you do. ⊗ Map G2 • 2-7-8 Moto-Asakusa, Taito-ku • 3834-2556 • ¥¥

Left **Homeikan Honkan** Center **Sawanoya Ryokan** Right **Ryokan Shigetsu**

TOP 10 Ryokan

1 Sukeroku no Yado Sadachiyo

A sophisticated, modern Japanese inn located just five minutes from the Senso-ji Temple *(see pp10–11)*. Japanese-style rooms come in different sizes. The staff are helpful, but not very fluent in English. Excellent communal Japanese bath. ✆ *Map R1 • 2-20-1 Asakusa, Taito-ku • 3842-6431 • www.sadachiyo.co.jp • ¥¥*

2 Ryokan Katsutaro

Seven Japanese-style rooms are provided at this friendly, family-run *ryokan*, situated in a quiet, traditional district near Ueno Park *(see pp16–17)*. Free Internet access available. ✆ *Map F1 • 4-16-8 Ikenohata, Taito-ku • 3821-9808 • www.katsutaro.com • ¥*

3 Ryokan Shigetsu

This beautifully maintained *ryokan* is adorned with paper screen windows and tatami mats. The two traditional baths here are a highlight, with views respectively of Senso-ji Temple and the city itself. ✆ *Map R2 • 1-31-1 Asakusa, Taito-ku • 3843-2345 • www.shigetsu.com • ¥¥*

4 Andon Ryokan

Enjoy the free tea and coffee here while taking in the compact design of this ultra-modern *ryokan*. Every room is equipped with Internet access, as well as a TV and DVD player. Showers on all floors and a communal Jacuzzi. English-speaking staff. ✆ *Map H1 • 2-34-10 Nihonzutsumi, Taito-ku • 3873-8611 • www.andon.co.jp • ¥¥*

5 Sawanoya Ryokan

A great place to meet fellow travelers, this long-established *ryokan* has been ever-popular with foreign guests. Rooms are small, but comfortable. There's a communal tub, though some rooms have en-suite baths. Situated in the interesting old quarter of Yanaka. Credit cards are not accepted. ✆ *Map F1 • 2-3-11 Yanaka, Taito-ku • 3822-2251 • ¥*

6 Suzuki Ryokan

Situated on the edge of Yanaka's romantic graveyard *(see pp26–7)*, this simple inn is run by elderly women who are very hospitable. They don't speak a word of English and the building is a bit rickety, but the pleasant surroundings more than make up for the inconvenience. ✆ *Map F1 • 7-15-23 Yanaka, Taito-ku • 3821-4944 • www.itcj.jp • ¥*

7 Meguro Gajoen

A cross between a high-end *ryokan* and luxury hotel, this place has walls and lounges all covered in original Japanese paintings and woodcarvings. The ambience exudes refinement, though bordering a little on the ostentatious. Both Western and Japanese rooms. ✆ *Map C2 • 1-8-1 Shimo Meguro, Meguro-ku • 3491-4111 • www.megurogajoen.co.jp • ¥¥¥¥*

8 Sansuiso Ryokan

An affordable choice in a rather expensive district. Some of the Japanese rooms have baths, others have communal facilities. Close to Gotanda Station. Note that there is a midnight curfew and credit cards are not accepted. ✆ *Map C2 • 2-9-5 Higashi-Gotanda, Shinagawa-ku • 3441-7475 • ¥¥*

9 Homeikan Honkan

Designated as an "important cultural property," this atmospheric old wooden *ryokan* has a small Japanese garden on the front. The inn's location in Hongo, a traditional neighborhood, enhances its charm. Communal bath. Credit cards are not accepted. ✆ *Map F2 • 5-10-5 Hongo, Bunkyo-ku • 3811-1181 • ¥¥*

10 Kimi Ryokan

Favored by budget travelers, this inn offers small, but immaculate, Japanese rooms. Bathing is communal. Friendly staff. Great value, so it's best to book ahead. ✆ *Map C1 • 2-36-8 Ikebukuro, Toshima-ku • 3971-3766 • www.kimi-ryokan.jp • ¥*

Unless otherwise stated, all hotels accept credit cards and have en-suite bathrooms and air conditioning.

Price Categories

For a standard, double room per night, including taxes and service charges.

¥	Under ¥8,000
¥¥	¥8,000–¥15,000
¥¥¥	¥15,000–¥25,000
¥¥¥¥	¥25,000–¥35,000
¥¥¥¥¥	Over ¥35,000

Hotel New Otani Tokyo

🔟 Hotels with Character

1 Nikko Kanaya Hotel

Built in 1873, this classic resort hotel presents an impressive blend of old-world charm and flawless service. Well-appointed rooms date from the Meiji era to the 1950s. Ⓢ Map B1 • 1300, Kami-Hatsuishi-machi, Nikko • 0288-54-0001 • www.kanayahotel.co.jp • ¥¥

2 Hill Top Hotel

An old favorite with writers, this prewar Art Deco hotel exudes charm and character. The older rooms are furnished with old-fashioned writing desks, while the more expensive suites have small, exquisite private gardens. Ⓢ Map E3 • 1-1 Kanda-Surugadai, Chiyoda-ku • 3293-2311 • www.yamanoue-hotel.co.jp • ¥¥¥

3 Arimax Hotel Shibuya

More like a private club than a hotel, this place is an island of European elegance, just minutes from the frenzy of Shibuya Crossing. Rooms feature luxurious furnishings. The Neoclassical decor is opulent but mellow. Ⓢ Map Q4 • 11-15 Kamiyama-cho, Shibuya-ku • 5454-1122 • www.arimaxhotelshibuya.co.jp • ¥¥¥¥

4 Hotel Okura

Full of old-fashioned grace, this hotel boasts Japanese decor, comfortable furnishings, a tea room and Japanese garden. Ⓢ Map K5 • 2-10-4 Toranomon, Minato-ku • 3582-0111 • www.okura.com/tokyo • ¥¥¥¥

5 Akasaka Prince Hotel

Featuring graceful lines, with European and modernist touches, this hotel was designed by the great Japanese architect Tange Kenzo. The public areas are resplendent with marble, steel, and glass, while the guest rooms are tastefully minimal. Ⓢ Map J3 • 1-2 Kioi-cho, Chiyoda-ku • 3234-1111 • www.princehotels.co.jp • ¥¥¥¥¥

6 Hotel New Otani Tokyo

Business tycoons, rock stars, and diplomats have stayed in this colossal hotel, which resembles a mini-city within the megalopolis. Lavishly furnished rooms and beautifully landscaped Japanese gardens add to the elegance. Ⓢ Map D4 • 4-1 Kioi-cho, Chiyoda-ku • 3265-1111 • www.1.newotani.co.jp • ¥¥¥¥¥

7 The Strings Hotel Tokyo

Located on the 26th floor, this hotel has scenic views of Odaiba Island and Rainbow Bridge (see pp28–9). The interior features natural sunlight, stone, wood, water, walnut furnishings, and low-slung sofas. Ⓢ Map C2 • Shinagawa East One Tower, 26-32F, 2-16-1 Konan, Minato-ku • 5783-1111 • www.intercontinental-strings.jp/english/index/html • ¥¥¥¥¥

8 Monterey Hanzomon Hotel

The rooms at this hotel blend traditional Japanese design with contemporary architecture, while the wall colors reflect the tastes of Edo-period samurai residences. Guests enjoy leisurely walks around the nearby Imperial Palace moats (see pp8–9). Ⓢ Map K1 • 23-1 Ichibancho, Chiyoda-ku • 3556-7111 • ¥¥¥

9 Four Seasons Hotel Chinzan-so

The lobby and corridors of this opulent hotel are decorated with original artwork. Its magnificent Japanese garden has some original features, including a wooden pagoda and Buddhist stone statuary. Rooms are immaculate. Ⓢ Map D1 • 2-10-8 Sekiguchi, Bunkyo-ku • 3943-2222 • www.fourseasons.com/tokyo • ¥¥¥¥¥

10 Fairmont Hotel

Located in the historical core of the city, this European-style hotel is characterized by an old-world calm and elegance. Handy for walks along the Imperial Palace moats and its landscaped outer gardens. Ⓢ Map K1 • 2-1-17 Kudan-minami, Chiyoda-ku • 3262-1151 • ¥¥¥

General Index

Acknowledgments

The Author
Stephen Mansfield is a British photo-journalist and author based in the Tokyo region. His work has appeared in more than 60 magazines, newspapers, and journals worldwide, including *The Geographical*, *South China Morning Post*, *The Traveller*, *Japan Quarterly*, and *Insight Japan*. He is a regular book reviewer for *The Japan Times*. His pieces cover a variety of subjects such as travel, contemporary issues, and cultural and literary themes. His photographs have appeared in several books. Stephen has authored ten books, including *Japan: Islands of the Floating World*, *Birmanie: Le Temps Suspendu*, and *China: Yunnan Province*. His latest book, *Japanese Stone Gardens*, was published in 2009.

Publisher Douglas Amrine

List Manager Christine Stroyan

Senior Editor Sadie Smith

Design Manager Sunita Gahir

Project Art Editors Nicola Erdpresser, Paul Jackson

Senior Cartographic Designer Casper Morris

Cartographer Maps produced by Simonetta Gori and Dominic Beddow of Draughtsman Ltd.

Photographer Martin Hladik

DTP Designers Natasha Lu, Jason Little

Production Controller Louise Minihane

Factchecker Katrina Grigg-Saito

Picture Credits
t-top; tl-top left; tlc-top left centre; tc-top centre; tr-top right; cla-centre left above; ca-centre above; cra-centre right above; cl-centre left; c-centre; cr-centre right; clb-centre left below; cb-centre below; crb-centre right below; bl-bottom left, b-bottom; bc-bottom centre; bcl-bottom centre left; br-bottom right; d-detail.

The Publisher would like to thank the following individuals, companies, and picture libraries for their kind permissions to reproduce their photographs.

ALAMY: Aflo Co. Ltd. 80-81; Tibor Bognar 10bc; Deco Images 10cb; Chris Hutty 11tl; Interfoto Pressebilda gentur 32bl; Arni Katz 6cr; John Lander 24-25c; Iain Masterton 51tr; Chris Porter 1c; Ulana Switucha 56tl; Jochen Tack 3tl.

Courtesy of BUNKAMURA: 96b.

CORBIS: amanaimages/Iwao Kataoka 12br; Bettman 33cl; Corbis Sygma/Annebicque 76tl; Corbis Sygma/Noboru Hashimoto 32tl; Jose Fuste Raga 30-31, 100-101.
EPA: Kimimasa Mayama 56tr, 57tl. Courtesy of FUJIYA HOTEL: 113tc.

Acknowledgments

Courtesy of HOTEL SEIYO GINZA: 126tc.

Courtesy of INAX GALLERY: 76tr.

Courtesy of JAPAN AIRLINES: 116tr.

Courtesy of PADDY FOLEY'S IRISH PUB: 42bl.

PHOTOLIBRARY: age fotostock/ Stefano Cellai 16-17c; DEA/G Sosio 55tl; Corbis/ Picture Net 3bl; Iconotec/Francois-Xavier Prevot 10-11c; Imagestate/Randa Bishop 78tl; Imagestate/Steve Vidler 8-9c; JTB Photo 22-23c, 68tl; Mauritus/Vidler Vidler 56bc.

Courtesy of SASAGIN: 42tl.

Courtesy of SHIN-YOKOHAMA RAMEN MUSEUM: 113tl.

Courtesy of TOKYO NATIONAL MUSEUM: 6br, 19tl, 35tr; *Domaru Armor* (15th century), a gift of Mr. Akita Kazusue 18c; *Warrior in Keiko-Style Armor* 18bc; *Tea Leaf Jar* (Edo period, 17th century) by Ninsei, Important Cultural Property 18crb; *Maple Viewers* (16th century) by Kano Hideyori, National Treasure 18-19c; *Lady Maya and Three Attendants* (7th century), Important Cultural Property 19cr; *Standing Bosatsu (Bodhisattva)* (13th century), Important Cultural Property 19bc; *Rikishi Mask, used for Gigaku dances* (8th century) 20c; *Ceramic Camel* (Tang dynasty, 8th century) 21c; *Seated Bodhisattva* (Kushan period, 2nd century, from Gandhara, Pakistan) 21cr.

VISAGE MEDIA SERVICES: Getty Images/Paul Chesley 120tl.

Phrase Book

The Japanese language is related to Okinawan and is similar to Altaic languages such as Mongolian and Turkish. Written Japanese uses a combination of three scripts: Chinese ideograms, known as *kanji*, and two syllable-based alphabet systems known as *hiragana* and *katakana*. These two latter are similar, *katakana* functioning as italics are used in English. Traditionally, Japanese is written in vertical columns from top right to bottom left, though the Western system is increasingly used. There are several romanization systems; the Hepburn system is used in this guide. To simplify romanization, macrons (long marks over vowels to indicate longer pronunciation) have not been used. Japanese pronunciation is fairly straightforward, and many words are "Japanized" versions of Western words. This Phrase Book gives the English word or phrase, followed by the Japanese script, then the romanization, adapted to aid pronunciation.

Guidelines for Pronunciation

When reading the romanization, give the same emphasis to all syllables. The practice in English of giving one syllable greater stress may render a Japanese word incomprehensible.

Pronounce vowels as in these English words:

a	as the "u" in "cup"
e	as in "red"
i	as in "chief"
o	as in "solid"
u	as the "oo" in "cuckoo"

When two vowels are used together, give each letter an individual sound:

ai	as in "pine"
ae	as if written "ah-eh"
ei	as in "pay"

Consonants are pronounced as in English. The letter *g* is always hard as in "gate," and *j* is always soft as in "joke." *R* is pronounced something between *r* and *l*. *F* is sometimes pronounced as *h*. "*Si*" always becomes "*shi*," but some people pronounce "*shi*" as "*hi*." *V* in Western words (e.g., "video") becomes *b*. If followed by a consonant, *n* may be pronounced as either *n* or *m*.

All consonants except *n* are always either followed by a vowel or doubled; however, sometimes an *i* or *u* is barely pronounced. In this Phrase Book, to aid pronunciation, apostrophes are used where an *i* or *u* is barely pronounced within a word, and double consonants where this occurs at the end of a word.

Dialects

Standard Japanese is used and understood throughout Japan by people of all backgrounds. But on a colloquial level, there are significant differences in both pronunciation and vocabulary, even between the Tokyo and Osaka-Kyoto areas, and rural accents are very strong.

Polite Words and Phrases

There are several different levels of politeness in the Japanese language, according to status, age, and situation. In everyday conversation, politeness levels are simply a question of the length of verb endings (longer is more polite), but in formal conversation entirely different words (*keigo*) are used. The level given in this Phrase Book is neutral yet polite.

In an Emergency

Help!	たすけて！	Tas'kete!
Stop!	とめて！	Tomete!
Call a doctor!	医者をよんで ください！	Isha o yonde kudasai!
Call an ambulance!	救急車を よんでください！	Kyukyusha o yonde kudasai!
Call the police!	警察を よんでください！	Keisatsu o yonde kudasai!
Fire!	火事！	Kaji!
Where is the hospital?	病院はどこに ありますか？	Byoin wa doko ni arimass-ka?
police box	交番	koban

Communication Essentials

Yes/no.	はい／いいえ	Hai/ie.
Thank you.	ありがとう。	Arigato.
Please (offering).	どうぞ。	Dozo.
Please (asking).	おねがいします。	Onegai shimass.
Do you speak English?	英語を 話せますか？	Eigo o hanasemass-ka?
I can't speak Japanese.	日本語は 話せません。	Nihongo wa hanasemasen.
Sorry/Excuse me!	すみません。	Sumimasen!
Could you help me please? (not emergency)	ちょっと手伝って いただけません か？	Chotto tets'datte itadakemasen-ka?

Useful Phrases

My name is	わたしの 名前は・・・ です。	Watashi no namae wa … dess.
How do you do, pleased to meet you.	はじめまして、 どうぞ よろしく。	Hajime-mash'te, dozo yorosh'ku.
How are you?	お元気ですか？	Ogenki dess-ka?
Good morning.	おはよう ございます。	Ohayo gozaimass.
Good afternoon/ good day.	こんにちは。	Konnichiwa.
Good evening.	こんばんは。	Konbanwa.
Good night.	おやすみなさい。	Oyasumi nasai.
Good-bye.	さよなら。	Sayonara.
What is (this)?	（これは）何 ですか？	(Kore wa) nan dess-ka?
Where can I get …?	・・・はどこに ありますか？	… wa doko ni arimass-ka?
How much is it?	いくらですか？	Ikura dess-ka?
What time is …?	・・・何時ですか？	… nan-ji dess-ka?
Cheers! (toast)	乾杯！	Kampai!
Where is the restroom/toilet?	お手洗い／おトイレ はどこ ですか？	Otearai/otoire wa doko dess-ka?
Here's my business card.	名刺をどうぞ。	Meishi o dozo.
How do you use this?	これをどうやって 使いますか？	Kore o doyatte ts'kaimass-ka?

Useful Words

I	わたし	watashi
woman	女性	josei
man	男性	dansei
wife	奥さん	ok'san
husband	主人	shujin
big/small	大きい／小さい	okii/chiisai
hot/cold	暑い／寒い	atsui/samui
warm	温かい	atatakai
good/	いい／よくない／	ii/yokunai/warui
not good/bad	悪い	
free (no charge)	ただ／無料	tada/muryo
here	ここ	koko
there	あそこ	asoko
this	これ	kore
that (nearby)	それ	sore
that (far away)	あれ	are
what?	何？	nani?
when?	いつ？	itsu?
why?	なぜ？／どうして？	naze?/dosh'te?
where?	どこ？	doko?
who?	誰？	dare?
which way?	どちら？	dochira?
enough	じゅうぶん／結構	jubun/kekko

Signs

open	営業中	eigyo-chu
closed	休日	kyujitsu
entrance	入口	iriguchi
exit	出口	deguchi
danger	危険	kiken
emergency exit	非常口	hijo-guchi
information	案内	annai
restroom, toilet	お手洗い／手洗い／	otearai/tearai/
	おトイレ／トイレ	otoire/toire
free (vacant)	空き	aki
men	男	otoko
women	女	onna

Money

Could you change this into yen please?	これを円に替えてください。	Kore o en ni kaete kudasai.
I'd like to cash these travelers' checks.	このトラベラーズチェックを現金にしたいです。	Kono toraberazu chekku o genkin ni shitai dess.
Do you take credit cards/travelers' checks?	クレジットカード／トラベラーズチェックで払えますか？	Kurejitto kado/toraberazu chekku de haraemass-ka?
bank	銀行	ginko
cash	現金	genkin
credit card	クレジットカード	kurejitto kado
currency exchange office	両替所	ryogaejo
dollars	ドル	doru
pounds	ポンド	pondo
yen	円	en

Keeping in Touch

Where is a telephone?	電話はどこにありますか？	Denwa wa doko ni arimass-ka?
May I use your phone?	電話を使ってもいいですか？	Denwa o ts'katte mo ii dess-ka?
Hello, this is ….	もしもし、…です。	Moshi-moshi, …dess.
I'd like to make an international call.	国際電話、お願いします。	Kokusai denwa, onegai shimass.
airmail	航空便	kokubin
e-mail	イーメール	i-meru
fax	ファクス	fak'su
postcard	ハガキ	hagaki
post office	郵便局	yubin-kyoku
stamp	切手	kitte
telephone booth	公衆電話	koshu denwa
telephone card	テレフォンカード	terefon kado

Staying in a Hotel

Do you have any vacancies?	部屋がありますか？	Heya ga arimass-ka?
I have a reservation.	予約をしてあります。	Yoyaku o sh'te arimass.
I'd like a room with a bathroom.	お風呂つきの部屋、お願いします。	Ofuro-ts'ki no heya, onegai shimass.
What is the charge per night?	一泊いくらですか？	Ippaku ikura dess-ka?
Japanese-style inn	旅館	ryokan
Japanese-style room	和室	wa-shitsu
key	鍵	kagi
front desk	フロント	furonto
single/twin room	シングル／ツイン	shinguru/tsuin
shower	シャワー	shyawa
Western-style hotel	ホテル	hoteru
Western-style room	洋室	yo-shitsu
Is tax included in the price?	税込みですか？	Zeikomi dess-ka?
Can I leave my luggage here for a little while?	荷物をちょっとここに預けてもいいですか？	Nimotsu o chotto koko ni azukete mo ii dess-ka?
air-conditioning	冷房／エアコン	reibo/eakon
bath	お風呂	ofuro
check-out	チェックアウト	chekku-auto

Eating Out

A table for one/two/three, please.	一人／二人／三人、お願いします。	Hitori/futari/sannin, onegai shimass.
May I see the menu.	メニュー、お願いします。	Menyu, onegai shimass.
Is there a set menu?	定食がありますか？	Teishoku ga arimass-ka?
I'd like ….	私は…がいいです。	Watashi wa … ga ii dess.
May I have one of those?	それをひとつ、お願いします。	Sore o hitotsu, onegai shimass.
I am a vegetarian.	私はベジタリアンです。	Watashi wa bejitarian dess.
Waiter/waitress!	ちょっとすみません。	Chotto sumimasen!
What would you recommend?	おすすめは何ですか？	Osusume wa nan dess-ka?
How do you eat this?	これはどうやって食べますか？	Kore wa doyatte tabemass-ka?
May I have the check please.	お勘定、お願いします。	Okanjo, onegai shimass.
May we have some more ….	もっと…、お願いします。	Motto …, onegai shimass.
The meal was very good, thank you.	ごちそうさまでした。おいしかったです。	Gochiso-sama desh'ta, oishikatta dess.
assortment	盛り合わせ	moriawase
boxed meal	弁当	bento
breakfast	朝食	cho-shoku
buffet	バイキング	baikingu
delicious	おいしい	oishii
dinner	夕食	yu-shoku
to drink	飲む	nomu
a drink	飲みもの	nomimono
to eat	食べる	taberu
food	食べもの／ごはん	tabemono/gohan
full (stomach)	おなかがいっぱい	onaka ga ippai
hot/cold	熱い／冷たい	atsui/tsumetai
hungry	おなかがすいた	onaka ga suita
Japanese food	和食	wa-shoku
lunch	昼食	chu-shoku

set menu	セット／定食	setto (snack)/teishoku (meal)
spicy	辛い	karai
sweet, mild	甘い	amai
Western food	洋食	yo-shoku
pepper	こしょう	kosho
salt	塩	shio
vegetables	野菜	yasai
sugar	砂糖	sato

Places to Eat

Cafeteria/canteen	食堂	shokudo
Chinese restaurant	中華料理屋	chuka-ryori-ya
coffee shop	喫茶店	kissaten
local bar	飲み屋／居酒屋	nomiya/izakaya
noodle stall	ラーメン屋	ramen-ya
restaurant	レストラン／料理屋	resutoran/ryori-ya
sushi on a conveyor belt	回転寿司	kaiten-zushi
upscale restaurant	料亭	ryotei
upscale vegetarian restaurant	精進料理屋	shojin-ryori-ya

Menu Decoder

ビール	biru	beer
ホットコーヒー	hotto-kohi	coffee (hot)
お茶	ocha	green tea
アイスコーヒー	aisu-kohi	iced coffee: black
アイスオーレ	kafe-o-re	with milk
レモンティー	remon ti	lemon tea
ミルク／牛乳	miruku/gyunyu	milk
ミネラルウォーター	mineraru uota	mineral water
酒	sake	rice wine
（甘酒）	(ama-zake)	(non-alcoholic)
紅茶	kocha	tea (Western-style)
ミルクティー	miruku ti	tea with milk
水	mizu	water
ウイスキー	uis'ki	whiskey
たけのこ	takenoko	bamboo shoots
とうふ	tofu	beancurd
もやし	moyashi	bean sprouts
豆	mame	beans
ビーフ／牛肉	bifu/gyuniku	beef
ふぐ	fugu	blowfish
かつお／ツナ	katsuo/tsuna	bonito, tuna
とり／鶏肉	tori/toriniku	chicken
かに	kani	crab
あひる	ahiru	duck
うなぎ	unagi	eel
たまご	tamago	egg
なす	nasu	eggplant/aubergine
みそ	miso	fermented soybean paste
納豆	natto	fermented soybeans
さしみ	sashimi	fish (raw)
油揚げ	abura-age	fried tofu
くだもの	kudamono	fruit
会席	kaiseki	haute cuisine
ニシン	nishin	herring
アイスクリーム	aisu-kurimu	ice cream
伊勢えび	ise-ebi	lobster
さば	saba	mackerel
肉	niku	meat
そば	soba	noodles: buckwheat
ラーメン	ramen	Chinese
うどん／そうめん	udon (fat)/somen (thin)	wheatflour
たこ	tako	octopus
カキ	kaki	oyster
つけもの	ts'kemono	pickles
豚肉	butaniku	pork
		rice:
ごはん	gohan	cooked
米	kome	uncooked
サラダ	sarada	salad
鮭	sake	salmon
ソーセージ	soseji	sausage
えび	ebi	shrimp
いか	ika	squid
鱒	masu	trout
ウニ	uni	sea urchin
すいか	suika	watermelon
ぼたん／いのしし	botan/inoshishi	wild boar
汁／スープ	shiru/supu	soup
しょうゆ	shoyu	soy sauce
スパゲティ	supageti	spaghetti
五目寿司	gomoku-zushi	sushi (mixed)

Numbers

0	ゼロ	zero
1	一	ichi
2	二	ni
3	三	san
4	四	yon/shi
5	五	go
6	六	roku
7	七	nana/shichi
8	八	hachi
9	九	kyu
10	十	ju
11	十一	ju-ichi
12	十二	ju-ni
20	二十	ni-ju
21	二十一	ni-ju-ichi
22	二十二	ni-ju-ni
30	三十	san-ju
40	四十	yon-ju
100	百	hyaku
101	百一	hyaku-ichi
200	二百	ni-hyaku
300	三百	san-byaku
400	四百	yon-hyaku
500	五百	go-hyaku
600	六百	ro-ppyaku
700	七百	nana-hyaku
800	八百	ha-ppyaku
900	九百	kyu-hyaku
1,000	千	sen
1,001	千一	sen-ichi
2,000	二千	ni-sen
10,000	一万	ichi-man
20,000	二万	ni-man
100,000	十万	ju-man
1,000,000	百万	hyaku-man

Time

Monday	月曜日	getsu-yobi
Tuesday	火曜日	ka-yobi
Wednesday	水曜日	sui-yobi
Thursday	木曜日	moku-yobi
Friday	金曜日	kin-yobi
Saturday	土曜日	do-yobi
Sunday	日曜日	nichi-yobi
minute	分	pun/fun
this year	今年	kotoshi
last year	去年	kyonen
next year	来年	rainen
one year	一年	ichi-nen
late	遅い	osoi
early	早い	hayai
soon	すぐ	sugu
one year	一年	ichi-nen

Selected Street and Sight Index

Index